Improving Behaviour and
Raising Self-Esteem
in the Classroom

Improving Behaviour and Raising Self-Esteem in the Classroom

A Practical Guide to Using Transactional Analysis

Giles Barrow, Emma Bradshaw and **Trudi Newton**

David Fulton Publishers
London

David Fulton Publishers Ltd
Ormond House, 26–27 Boswell Street, London WC1N 3JZ

www.fultonpublishers.co.uk

First published in Great Britain by David Fulton Publishers 2001

British Library Cataloguing in Publication Data
A catalogue record for this book is available from the British Library

ISBN 1–85346–775–8

The publishers would like to thank Lyn Corson for copy-editing and Sally Critchlow for proofreading this book.

Typeset by Elite Typesetting Techniques, Eastleigh, Hampshire
Printed in Great Britain by The Cromwell Press Ltd, Trowbridge, Wilts.

Contents

Acknowledgements

In writing this book we have drawn on ideas from many writers, colleagues and friends who use Transactional Analysis (TA) and have applied them in ways that we hope will be effective for schools. We are especially grateful to Jean Illsley Clarke and to Julie Hay for the generosity with which they have both encouraged us in using and adapting their material, and for the inspiration and support they have given us.

We also want to thank Carole Gesme, Steve Karpman, Adrienne Lee, Pat Daunt and Ginty Furmage for permission to include pieces from their work.

Another group to whom thanks are due are those teachers and others who work in schools who have shared with us, and allowed us to quote, examples of how they have applied in school what they have learned from us in workshops and in-service education and training (INSET); and the pupils who have helped us to see the power and potential of the 'tools' in real use. Special thanks to Hatfeild School, John Gray, Jane Keary, Jill Lowe and Linda Hellaby.

At David Fulton Publishers, Jude Bowen and Margaret Haigh have always been available and helpful, and most importantly, encouraged us enormously.

TA is a very visual system and three people have contributed to the visual aspects of this book: David Newton created the diagrams and tables, Clive Goddard the cartoons and illustrations, and Rosie Barrow the drawings at the end of Chapter 5 and in the final chapter. Our thanks to all of them.

And a big 'thank you' to Jackie, Mick and David, and to Sara and her family for the days in Suffolk which made all the difference!

For ourselves, we have shared: structuring the writing process, encouraging each other, problem solving together, working cooperatively and most of all enjoying lots of fun and positive strokes.

Giles Barrow, Emma Bradshaw
and Trudi Newton
July 2001

CHAPTER 1

Introduction

- What do you expect from this book?
- What do the authors of this book expect of you?
- What do the publishers expect of you the reader, and us the authors?

This book is about behaviour; in our view as authors behaviour is about communication between people in a context or environment. A major factor in our communication and relationship with others is how we contract with them, and whether we do this implicitly or explicitly. So this book is going to start with a contract (contracting will be dealt with in more detail in Chapter 3). However, we hope that by making this contract explicit it will be clear that the value of this book will be dependent on each party keeping their side of the contract. The reader will only get as much out of the book as they are prepared to apply, try out and understand its ideas. This can only happen if the authors and the publishers have done their part in making the book accessible and relevant.

It is also important to be clear about what each party can offer as well as expect.

- The authors have some information, concepts and ideas that they want to share with a broad audience.
- The publishers have a service to offer to readers. They have an organisation which is capable of delivering information to a broad audience.
- The readers have the potential to take, use and spread the concepts and ideas of the authors to affect the schools and pupils they work in and with.

Below is another way of looking at the questions or expectations given at the start of this chapter (Figure 1.1). Each side of the triangle represents two-way expectations.

Reader–Publisher expectations:

- The readers expect the publishers to provide up-to-date and relevant book titles of a high standard and professional quality. They also expect a range of titles to be produced on different topics – and behaviour is a topic that has

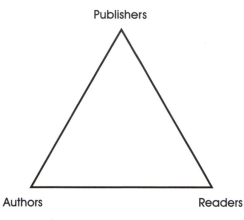

Figure 1.1 The three-cornered contract

been increasingly sought after by readers. They expect the book to be good value for money and to be readable. The publishers expect the readers to buy the book, to use it and to tell their friends about it. The publishers also expect to get paid for the production of books and to make a reasonable profit on each one sold.

Author–Reader expectations:

- The authors expect the readers to use the book to help them to understand behaviour and self-esteem, then to use and apply the information to develop their skills and practice. The readers expect the authors to provide information in the book in a way that can be easily understood and applied to school life. They expect to get good value for money from the book and want it to provide information that they do not have already.

Author–Publisher expectations:

- The authors expect the publishers to print and distribute the book. They expect the book to be marketed and printed true to their manuscript with suggestions for improvements, correcting any errors and ensuring the layout is both sensible and attractive. They also expect to get paid a royalty on the sale of each book. The authors expect their book and message to receive the wider audience to which the publishers have access. The publishers expect the authors to write the book on time. They expect the authors to provide material that further develops their range of books and broadens their title list. They expect the book to be good enough to make them a profit on their outlay.

The wider context

Every contract is set in a wider context and the publishers hope that this title will be a valuable contribution to the debate on the issue of understanding and responding to difficult behaviour. As authors we are well aware of the substantial demand for training, support and resources relating to pupil behaviour. It is a theme high on the national agenda, reflected not only in the media but also in the wide range of government initiatives, guidance and legislation.

Central policies regarding social inclusion have generated a significant increase in interest and funding for programmes that span a wide spectrum of activity in key departments including education, health, community development and youth justice. More specifically, in the education field there has been a series of developments, many of which have been branded under individual programmes, including: *Sure Start, Connexions, On Track, Crime Reduction in Secondary Schools, Healthy Schools.*

Running in parallel has been the emergence of new guidance, some of which is underpinned by changes in legislation. Readers may be familiar with a number of related issues covered by official publications over the past few years including: target setting for pupils with social, emotional and behavioural needs (Qualifications and Curriculum Authority/Department for Education and Employment (QCA/DfEE) 2000), specialist standards for teachers (Teacher Training Agency (TTA) 1999), revised arrangements for special educational needs (DfEE 2000) and social inclusion (DfEE 1999).

One of the consequences of the major policy shift towards social inclusion has been a renewed pressure on schools to consider issues of pupil behaviour. The emphasis on increasing the inclusive capacity of schools is without doubt a challenging agenda, and some might argue that it is an impossible one. With targets to reduce truancy and exclusion, an expectation that specialist providers review their role within local contexts and an awareness of the impact of education failure in later adult life, schools are increasingly under pressure to explore how this might all be achieved.

Not surprisingly many schools have pointed out some of the inherent tensions in the central social inclusion policy. The shift towards inclusion is arguably undermined by the long-standing pupil achievement agenda where the emphasis has been on increasing academic standards, publication of 'comparative' school performance and a free-market approach to school admissions, most of which have been enforced through the inspectorate system.

All in all it has been difficult for schools to reconcile inclusive aspirations with the realities of a limited standards agenda. Conflicts within government guidance and competing legislative priorities have not helped to support schools. In particular, working towards a coherent approach to raising education standards for an increasingly wide range of pupils has often meant having to make a decision between meeting either one or other of the policy agendas.

We believe, sadly, that as a consequence of this apparent tension in policy, there is a limited range of outcomes. Teachers can feel faced with a situation in which either children must be to blame for difficult behaviour, or they as teachers are somehow to blame – a perspective that some smaller-minded national papers seem to favour. This position – that it must be either children or teachers that are to blame – is both negative and unsustainable. Our position is that it is very rare that either children or teachers fail; they simply do not. What fails both teachers and children are the perspectives that we use to get us out of difficulty. This observation lies at the heart of our hopes for this book and in the work that takes place in schools.

We are well aware that one of the objections raised by schools is that there are too many children that are 'beyond'; that there is a growing number of youngsters for whom the 'normal', mainstream approaches to managing behaviour simply do not work. Invariably the perspectives used in understanding and responding to these cases are drawn from classic cognitive/behavioural theory – the standard, default mode for many schools.

As part of our contract with the readership for this book, we invite you to consider the possibility that the children beyond are actually telling us something about the limitations of conventional response to difficult behaviour. Techniques that may seem to 'work' for many children for much of the time may leave us bereft of ideas and success when it come to those most difficult cases. The outcome can be to condemn kids – and that can hold only fears for the future. The notion that instead we condemn adults in schools for not doing it right is equally futile – they are our best hope. In responding to the challenge of increasing the inclusive capacity of schools, we need to take a more critical look at the theory, technique and practice of what we do in schools.

In our work with schools we have noticed a common theme. In working on pupil behaviour the conventional approaches continue to make their mark. Colleagues welcome being reminded of the need to create structure through reinforcement and use consequence to discourage unwanted behaviours and recognise the impact of thinking on changing behaviour. Often colleagues present instances where the approaches fall short of success, and they need reminding that relying on a single perspective limits effective work with children.

Where we have started to introduce concepts drawn from Transactional Analysis (TA), something else happens. As an alternative model it illustrates, through familiar experience, new ways of understanding behaviour and of creating different insights into challenging situations.

What has TA got to offer education?

We started with a day's training for our team, using a few concepts from the TA approach. This led to further training and reading as the real implications of the ideas began to germinate. The concepts were easy to understand and use straight away and with practice they became more powerful. The more that was learnt, the more could be applied; yet a little was also enough to use. TA concepts can be taught in 30 minutes or developed over a number of days, are easily learned (by children as well as adults) and easy to apply. They are particularly good at helping to unravel the complex way humans communicate, so helping us to move forward and look at the way things could be better and less confused. This is why this book has been written – to make TA more accessible to mainstream educators.

It is because of our experience in introducing TA to schools that we have begun to recognise that it is an approach that can make a serious impact on how schools respond to the complexities of the central emphasis on social inclusion. Some of the ways in which TA helpfully contributes to school life are by:

- Promoting discussion and confidence in developing emotional literacy among staff and pupils.
- Providing a framework for managing conflict.
- Presenting an alternative model for understanding and using praise.
- Ensuring effective arrangements for working in partnerships with parents, pupils and other agencies.
- Building pupils' confidence in responding to the challenges of learning.
- Promoting the mental health of both adults and children in schools.

What makes TA such an effective approach?

One way of describing TA is as a tree (Figure 1.2).

Like any tree it has *roots* which go deep into the ground; in this case the ground of psychodynamic theory, ascribing a person's current attitudes and behaviour to early experience and interactions with others, whether positive or negative. Eric Berne, the originator of TA, was a psychiatrist and psychotherapist who had trained with Erik Erikson. Working with groups in the 1950s he studied intuition and observed behaviour to develop the concepts and visual models that became the core of TA theory. Berne himself practised and wrote about TA as a psychotherapy until his death in 1970, while others saw the potential application of his theories to organisations and education, and began to extend the areas in which TA can be used. Berne's preferred description of TA was a 'social psychology' and/or a 'social psychiatry'; a method by which observations of behaviour could be used to infer thinking and feeling, and insight into 'what makes people tick'.

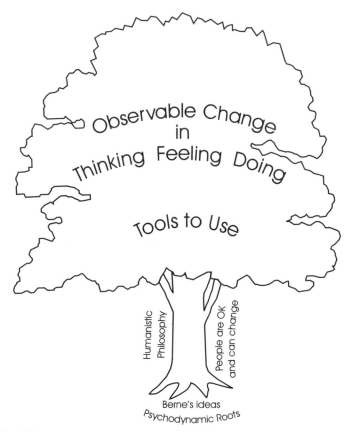

Figure 1.2 The TA tree

A tree also has a *trunk*, which gives it shape and structure, and through which nutrients pass from the ground to the leaves, flowers and fruit. The products of photosynthesis in the leaves return to nourish all parts of the tree and enable it to grow and become stronger and more robust. The trunk of the TA tree is a humanistic philosophy that maintains that every individual is intrinsically valuable, important and worthy of respect. Colloquially this has become known as 'I'm OK, you're OK' or more accurately 'I am OK with myself and you are OK with me; I respect and accept myself and you, and trust you to do the same to me'. The subtext of this belief is that when we behave towards those around us 'as if' we and they are 'OK' we invite 'OK-ness' in them. Teasing out the implications of this philosophy we can say that everyone (except the seriously brain damaged) can think for themselves, make decisions, problem solve, grow and change. People may, and often do, behave in 'not-OK' ways; this behaviour is the result of using ineffective strategies for communication and interaction which, with an OK–OK approach and the right information, can be changed.

The hope and optimism of this approach is manifested in its accessibility. Berne said 'If something can't be understood by an intelligent eight year old it isn't worth saying' (Steiner 2001). He opposed professional elitism and the use of complex language. When he was accused of over-simplifying concepts he responded 'those who want to make things difficult can sit at the over-complicated table over there; those who want to understand what's going on can join me at the over-simplified table over here' (Steiner 2001). The straightforwardness, immediacy and appeal of TA ideas have sometimes led to accusations of superficiality and TA being regarded as a 'pop psychology'. This is unfortunate, and misleading, when such responses prevent people from appreciating the sound theory and creative, flexible application which are characteristic of TA writers and practitioners. The *language* of TA, and the terms used, *are* simple, and easy to understand; this is part of its accessibility and attractiveness.

The life and health of a tree can be seen in what it produces – its *foliage, flowers and fruit.* The roots and trunk are there to make these possible. Products of the TA tree include observable change in thinking, feeling and behaviour. These are the purpose of the tree's existence, its reason for being. As well as bringing about change in people, TA as a system grows, changes and develops as new ideas emerge and are integrated into the basic theory. This is the nourishment that returns from the foliage to the roots and feeds the expanding trunk. TA is, above all, a theory of how personality develops, how human beings communicate, and how we can take charge of that to bring about desired changes – for individuals, relationships, groups, organisations and even whole societies.

Summary

TA is a coherent theoretical approach which includes understanding causes, operating from an ethical, values-based position, and enabling behavioural change. It therefore integrates elements of psychodynamic, behavioural, systemic and cognitive perspectives as a single congruent system; it provides a framework that can encompass a number of models.

- It offers a range of *tools and strategies* that can be learned and are effective in improving communication at all levels.
- It provides a *language* through which people can learn to describe their experience; like any new language it takes practice at first, and practice leads to increasing fluency.
- It is a *decisional model* through which people can choose what, when and if they want to change; this is linked to a contractual approach of mutual and self-esteem and clarity of purpose.
- As a *practical educational psychology* it can lead to growth and development for teachers, pupils and schools.

Using this book

The chapters of this book interlock with each other like a jigsaw. They make reference to each other, and the concepts in each complement and expand as the book develops. The book starts with a focus on individual relationships and ends with considering the whole school as an organisation. This is because, in our experience, it is often the immediate one-to-one relationships that dwell on our minds. However, the final chapter is in many respects the most important; if positive change is to be maintained, a whole-school approach is crucial.

'*I spend so much of my time with a small number of pupils sorting out their conflicts with other pupils and teachers*' (heard from many year leaders). Chapter 2 deals with issues around conflict. How does conflict occur? What is it? How is it best dealt with?

'*You can put him on a behaviour contract but it won't work.*' (special educational needs coordinator (SENCO)). Contracting is the focus of Chapter 3 and follows neatly on from conflict as, if it is used effectively, it can be one of the best methods to prevent difficulties. We look at the theories that underpin contracts and consider practical examples of how it can be used in school. This chapter will help to dispel some myths about what is and what isn't a contract.

'*Teacher self-esteem is at an all-time low – who in their right mind would want to train as a teacher?*' (heard in many staffrooms – but not all). Chapter 4 looks at one of the biggest causes of conflict: low self-esteem. This is also one of the biggest obstacles that gets in the way of learning. We look at the way pupils and adults feel about themselves as this has a significant impact on the risks they are prepared to take in life and learning.

'*I'm always amazed at how some of the most troubled youngsters can be brilliant at helping out in the nursery*' (class teacher). Chapter 5 describes the way people develop and grow emotionally from infancy to adulthood. Understanding the process of emotional growth helps us to identify gaps in development. This can then help to assess what support can be provided to meet individual needs. This chapter looks at those messages that need to be heard at various stages of development, giving us ways that can start to fill those missing gaps.

'*The kids here are really needy and staff get on really well together, we have to laugh sometimes or we'd cry.*' As authors we believe that staff teams that work together and support each other result in effective schools. Chapter 6 pulls the book together by looking at school culture. What makes a well-balanced school, a school that supports all its pupils and staff in their development and education? How can we assess where we are at as an institution and what can we do to become more balanced? This final chapter is in effect the most important as it is only through establishing healthy school systems that effective change can be sustained.

Healthy young people make good employees, parents and community members. This, in the broadest sense, is the harvest of getting education right. The emphasis on literacy, numeracy and the academic in schools is only in balance if we include emotional literacy. This book is designed to be a resource for emotional growth and development. The impact on school achievement of emotionally healthy pupils is that achievement will rise in proportion to that emotional well-being. Risks will only be taken in learning when people feel safe taking them. Real and lasting learning involves risk taking.

We also hope that, by gaining more understanding through this book, many of the things that have 'felt right' in the past will now have the theory to underpin why they felt right and worked. This then gives justification to use. This accountability is vital in schools, where every minute spent has to be accounted for. This is not meant to devalue the learning of basic skills, just to redress the balance. Children will be able to learn effectively when they have the emotional capacity to do so, and the curriculum including literacy and numeracy and emotional development is vital for a child's future. One without the other is not effective. The message we are getting from the workplace is that what is required is a balance – employers are looking for people who can work in teams, problem solvers and good communicators who also have good basic skills in literacy, numeracy and information technology (IT). The truth, as always, does not lie in one way or another but in a balance.

Our vision for the future of TA in education is that it should become a mainstream tool for all teachers. The basics of TA should be taught to all teachers – and in particular those in training. The understanding of communication is the best way any teacher can be equipped. Good communication leads to effective learning, whatever the subject. It will also lead to teachers feeling empowered to deal with and unravel behaviour difficulties, rather than feeling that they don't have the skills. More than anything, TA is about can do rather than can't do. For too long teachers have been told they can't and don't do. The truth is that they can, given the right tools to use and support to develop their skills. TA is an approach that can offer this.

To help readers find their way around the book we have chosen a symbol to represent each chapter (Figure 1.3).

Dealing with Conflict

Partnership Planning: Contracting in Schools

Raising Self-Esteem

Emotional Development

Developing a Positive School Culture

Figure 1.3 Chapter symbols

How to use the book

- Read it from cover to cover.
- Dip in and out.
- Come back to it with a problem.
- Lend it to colleagues.
- Take bite-size chunks and practise using them.
- Teach the ideas to some children.
- Observe behaviour and test it out.
- Challenge it, try to find gaps.
- Revisit regularly.
- Attend a course or further training.
- Have fun with it.
- Use it as prevention not just cure.

More than anything enjoy it and write to tell us about how you have used it.

CHAPTER 2

Dealing with Conflict

- How much time do you spend caught up in conflict that you never planned?
- How does it happen?
- Are you looking for different ways to respond?

In this section we will look at conflict and its effect on relationships in and around the classroom and school. The use of TA to understand conflict will be introduced through the concepts of egostates, transactions and games, and how they appear in terms of people's behaviour. The understanding of what happens when we get drawn into conflict will be used to examine how conflict can be avoided. Avoiding conflict saves time in the end, even if initially time needs to be invested to find alternative ways of dealing with difficulties. Stress can also be avoided, which is one of the most common causes of teacher absence in schools today and is clearly unhelpful for pupils too.

Some of the most stressful times we spend in school are the ones when we haven't got the time, so we take short cuts. In relationships that means we often end up in conflict with someone simply because we don't take the time to communicate effectively with them. The consequence of this is that we then have to spend more time sorting it out. In schools, where time is so precious, we don't have the time for conflict.

People who are familiar with conflict can often find themselves playing a game of conflict and invariably they are well rehearsed. Those colleagues, pupils and parents with whom we tend to get into conflict can be well used to it and draw us in before we have had time to think. Before we know where we are, we find we have achieved little of what we set out to achieve.

An example from a form tutor – 'I just needed to talk to Tom's mum about his lack of PE kit and I find myself defending the decision to put Tom in detention for the lack of his PE kit. How did I end up here?' Understanding what went wrong can help us avoid further conflict and respond differently in future situations.

So often in these scenarios we end up feeling like a victim and it is always easy to think of others as 'unreasonable' or 'aggressive' – as in the cartoon (Figure 2.1).

Figure 2.1

How many times have you found yourself in a win–lose situation as illustrated here? With younger children it might also be those 'Oh no you won't – Oh yes I will' type conversations.

Introducing egostates

In TA language a person can be described as having three egostates: Parent, Adult and Child (Figure 2.2). These form three parts of our personality and their content is unique to each individual. More accurately we can be said to have three *sets* of egostates developed over time as our experience of the world grows. We all have these, whatever age we are, and we all began to develop them when we were very small as different ways of processing and categorising reality. Putting things into categories appears to be one of the earliest 'ways of thinking' that we can observe in young babies – as young as a few days (Gopnik *et al.* 1999). As we record what happens to us and around us we develop an image of ourselves. The *subjective* aspect of our experience becomes the Child set of egostates related to various stages of our development. Our probability estimating and *objectivity* forms our Adult; and our *relationship* to others, and our imitation and modelling of them, becomes our Parent set of egostates, which may include things derived from many different people around us. In this book, as in all TA writing, Parent, Adult and Child are written with capital initial letters when they refer to egostates, to distinguish them from parents (mothers, fathers and other care-givers), adults (grown-ups) and children.

We can summarise by saying that the Parent consists of all the behaviours, thinking and feeling that we have copied from the 'big people' around us. The Child consists of the behaviours, thinking and feeling we experienced when young and may replay in the present, and the Adult consists of the behaviours, thinking

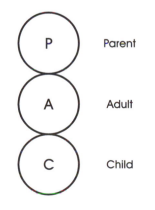

Figure 2.2 Egostate diagram (Berne 1961)

and feeling appropriate to the here and now (Stewart and Joines 1987). As we develop our egostates, during childhood and beyond, through interaction with others, some parts may become 'fixed', while others are more open to change as we encounter new and different experiences.

Just as we have three categories of 'content' derived from our experience (known as the 'structure' of our personality), so we have three corresponding categories of functioning in the present. The Parent category is about how we take responsibility for ourselves and others. This is diagrammed as divided into two parts: Controlling Parent and Nurturing Parent on Figure 2.3. These describe two functions of the Parent egostate – control and care. The behaviours derived from

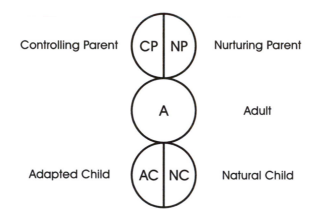

Figure 2.3 Functional egostate diagram (Berne 1961)

each can be positive and beneficial, or negative and limiting. These are known as *modes* of behaviour (Lapworth *et al.* 1995; Temple 1999a). Following Clarke (Clarke and Dawson 1998) we use the terms Structuring and Nurturing (positive), and Critical and Marshmallowy (negative) for these (see Figure 2.4). Similarly the Child category, which is about how we express our own unique identity, is divided into Adapted and Natural Child: the first because it concerns our behaviour in response to demands from other people; the second a 'free' expression of our wants and needs. Again, each can be shown by behaviour which is positive or negative; we use the terms Cooperative and Spontaneous (positive) (Temple 1999a) and Compliant/Rebellious or Immature (negative). Both compliant and rebellious behaviour are negative manifestations of the Adapted Child; rebel behaviour is more likely to be a problem for teachers while compliance may go unnoticed. It should not be mistaken for cooperation; the descriptions in Table 2.1 make the difference clear. Adult functioning can be called 'accounting' mode

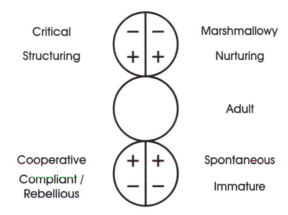

Figure 2.4 Behavioural modes

(Temple 1999a) when it is about reality assessment, awareness of self and others, and making sense of what is going on. As we take account of all the factors affecting a situation we may choose to respond from any appropriate positive mode. Sometimes Adult can be *too* 'detached' and another mode might provide a more appropriate response.

How we act in relation to others – our interactions, communication (or lack of it) – can be described in terms of the modes, and will partly depend on the beliefs, strategies, models and 'recording' that comprise our egostates. Sometimes our negative behaviours may be the result of a lack of learning, or of awareness of options or strategies. We can change this in the present and learn new ways of acting, to switch to positive alternatives to improve communication and effectiveness. Similarly, just as we can learn new ways of behaving, we can update the content of our egostates by taking on board new information or different approaches, and by checking out – and if necessary changing – our beliefs about ourselves and others. This is a dynamic process, not a once-and-for-all programming.

Teachers we have known in the past will have influenced our Parent thinking, feeling and behaving; our own experiences of school will have formed part of our Child egostate – all of these will affect which modes we consciously or unconsciously choose to use in teaching. A well-functioning Adult will consistently integrate relevant information from our Parent and Child with that from the environment and respond appropriately in the here and now by choosing and using a positive mode that has a good chance of being effective in the circumstances. When this doesn't happen we may react automatically, as if replaying a scene from the past, and lose effectiveness by failing to take into account all the aspects of the here and now situation.

Look at Table 2.1 and think of examples of times when you have behaved in each of the ways described.

MODE	ATTITUDE	WORDS	POSTURE, ETC.	EXAMPLE
Critical	fault finding, adversarial, expect obedience, punitive, know best, threats, warnings	'have to' 'should' 'must' 'never'	standing over, wag finger, hands on hips, condescending, frowning	'Get out of my classroom – you never do as you're told – and don't bother coming back until you can behave'
Structuring	firm, inspiring, empowering, set limits, show expectations, give security, keep boundaries	'will' 'expect' (clear)	controlled, solid, boundaried, focused, decisive	'Billy you know the rule about talking when I'm talking, please listen so you will know what to do next'
Marshmallowy	fussing, over-protective, smothering, over-indulgent, sugary, too close	'let me' 'poor thing' 'I'll help you'	soothing, touching, leaning over someone	'Don't worry if you can't do it Billy, I know you're having a bad time at home'
Nurturing	encouraging, empathic, accepting, appreciative, understanding, available	'like' 'care' 'well done' 'do you want my help?'	open posture, smiling, concerned/ comforting	'Billy I know it's difficult to concentrate, come on, I'll help you get started'
Adult	aware, objective, logical, practical, alert, thoughtful, receptive	'how' (questions, discussion)	relaxed, interested, observant, eye contact	'OK, Billy, the rest of us are trying to get on with the work. Do you want to carry on here and finish it, or carry on at break-time with me?'
Cooperative	friendly, considerate, assertive, diplomatic, respectful, confident	'please' 'thanks' 'help' (asking, listening)	attentive, restrained, polite, willing, sharing	'What is it you need help with, Billy? Well done for putting your hand up'
Compliant/ Rebellious	conforming, anxious, pleasing, whiny withdrawn/obstinate, rebellious, defiant, aggressive	'can't' 'won't' 'try' 'wish'	collapsed, closed, pouting, demanding, swearing, shouting	'No, you can't go to the toilet! I'm fed up with you mucking about in my classes'
Spontaneous	playful, creative, energetic, vital, expressive, motivated, curious	'wow' 'great' 'fun' 'want'	loose, unselfconscious, enthusiastic, head on one side, happy	'Right, come on, you lot. Let's have a race. Whoever gets the answer to question two first can choose what we do for the last five minutes'
Immature	irresponsible, selfish, careless, inconsiderate, thoughtless	'won't' 'me' 'my' 'no'	out of control, inappropriate, emotional, over loud	'Well, let them wait in the cold. I've got my coffee to finish'

Table 2.1 Characteristics of modes

Identifying transactions

Which modes were the teacher and pupil coming from in the cartoon earlier in the chapter (Figure 2.1)? The language can give us useful clues as to the mode the characters are using:

Teacher – 'Sit down, I'm trying to start the lesson.' This is a direct instruction and taken as such comes from Structuring Parent. The response of the pupil is to sit on the chair with her coat on. This gesture is coming from the Rebel Child as the flat refusal 'No!' Rebel Child is one part of Adapted Child. If you are operating in Adapted Child you either do as asked or you rebel. In this scenario the pupil is very much rebelling.

Each time we communicate with someone else we take part in a *transaction*. The transactions in this conflict are *complementary* and they can go on and on ad infinitum. Every transaction consists of a stimulus and a response; these are diagrammed as arrowed lines (see Figure 2.5). In a complementary transaction the lines are parallel; the egostate addressed is the one that responds.

Parent and Child modes appeal to each other like magnets. Adult appeals to Adult. Often teachers feel that they are in charge but when a pupil tries to communicate with a teacher from a negative Child mode then they appeal to the negative Parent of the teacher. Before the teacher has had time to think they are drawn into a conflict by reacting to the offending pupil in a negative Parent mode. The transaction was started by the pupil who hooked the teacher's Parent – so, who is in control after all?

If the conflict in the cartoon were to be translated into transactions, each frame would look the same as the same transaction is being repeated each time. It's like a game of tennis, with the verbal ball being bounced between Critical Parent and

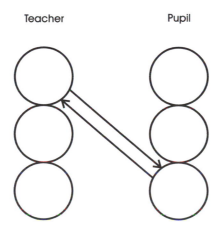

Figure 2.5 Transactional diagram: a Parent–Child transaction

Figure 2.6

Rebel Child. The words and gestures change and the stakes continue to rise, but the type of transaction remains constant until, in the last frame, someone leaves the room (Figure 2.6). Then we see a different type of transaction, known as a *crossed transaction*; this usually results in stopping the communication in some way, and something different will happen.

- What is the solution to stopping the conflict?
- What could the teacher or pupil have done differently to avoid the conflict?
- What could either do to get out of it once it had started?

The transactions in most of the scenario are complementary or parallel. To change the outcome someone must redirect the ball, or 'cross' the transaction. This means responding from a different mode, and thereby inviting a different response from the other person. In the cartoon the crossed transaction may have brought that particular scenario to an end but it is unlikely to have been resolved effectively. We can also cross transactions in a positive way; here are some possible options.

The teacher could have noticed that the pupil was looking upset and therefore ignored her until the lesson was started and then approached with an 'Are you OK?' This response would still have been from the Parent but it would have been from the nurturing side. The pupil may well have stayed in Child but have responded from Natural Child and been able to talk about her feelings or the reason for her lateness, or switched to cooperative mode and decided to do as asked in response to the teacher's concern. This approach also gives the pupil space to settle down.

The teacher could have ignored the behaviour because he suspected that particular pupil of looking for an argument. This response would have come from the Adult using logical thinking in the here and now. When that decision has been made it is not a case of letting the pupil off the hook, but of taking the decision to tackle that particular infringement of school or class rules at a different time or in a different way. All behaviour communicates something to us, so to ignore or push it aside completely will also cost us time in the future. We all need to learn that there are consequences to our behaviour to help us learn and develop. To a person well practised in conflict an alternative consequence to a head-to-head row will be remembered. A consequence of not following up an incident might result in even more disruptive behaviour next time, just to see how far it could go before a reaction is reached. The answer so often lies in the middle ground, and different approaches are needed for different pupils, parents and teachers at different times. A little time invested now will save a lot of time later on.

Another example from the same incident might be that the teacher leaves the pupil with her coat on rocking on her chair. Once the lesson has started the teacher goes up to the pupil and says 'I need you to take your coat off and start to do this work. If you choose to stay here and do nothing then I will speak to you at break-time. If you cannot do the work because something is bothering you then you may go and speak to the school nurse or your Head of Year.' In a primary school the teacher may make an agreement to speak to the child at break. These responses are not about giving in to a pupil's infringement of a school rule; instead they offer an alternative response that enables the teacher to continue pursuing their core task of teaching the class. It is also a response that will be seen by the rest of the class as the teacher dealing with that pupil. This is often a concern for teachers – that they should not be seen as giving in. Boundaries are important to all of us and there need to be identified consequences for actions. This can be done in a non-confrontational way, which is more effective because over time it is less stressful and quicker.

Teachers will feel differently about the extent to which they can respond to difficulties in the classroom and much of this will be determined by the context of the school. In training many teachers tell us that ignoring low-level difficulties is risky because if a senior teacher should pass by and see the infringement they might either undermine the teacher by intervening unnecessarily, or chastise the teacher! There are a number of issues around how school culture affects the capacity of adults and children to be flexible in responding to difficulty. This aspect of school life is considered in the next chapter, in which we introduce the idea of negotiated class, school and individual contracts, and in the final chapter in which we explore the impact of school ethos on everyday situations.

Why are some people better at conflict than others?

Some people are better at conflict than others because they have had more practice at it.

Case study

Jim is eleven years old. He lives with Mum and her boyfriend. Jim only does what his mother's boyfriend wants because he knows that if he doesn't, he gets hit hard. His mother's boyfriend only communicates with Jim from a negative Critical Parent mode.

Jim is used to being in Child; often he is in compliant Adapted Child and has to do as his mother's boyfriend tells him. This means that he is very well practised at being in Child and therefore he tends to communicate to others from there. Sometimes he bullies other pupils, thus repeating a pattern of what happens to him. However Jim finds it hard to communicate with others from Adult as he has had very little practice at using Adult; nor has he seen it in the people closest to him. Logic and self-control are not things Jim is used to encountering. When he comes to school the automatic reaction he attracts is Critical Parent from teachers around him. All they do is reinforce the ways of communication he is well practised in from his home experiences. He is very good at conflict and often is happier to use his Rebel Child because he knows he won't get hit at school.

Just because Jim's use of Adult is limited does not mean that he cannot be helped to practise it and develop it (like a muscle that needs exercise to grow). He needs good role models who do not pick up on his invitations to a negative Parent–Child transaction. He needs to be given opportunities to learn to think for himself and take responsibility for his actions. He needs to be provided with opportunities to develop these skills, but is often denied these as he is seen as not able. Therefore the cycle continues. Jim needs to learn to use and develop his Adult, he needs to develop from where he is and he needs lots of practice.

How can we give Jim the practical help he requires?

- Give him choice about consequences related to his actions – Jim was given the option of completing work and getting time on the computer or staying in at break to finish work.
- Target his behaviour not him – Jim was rewarded every time he put his hand up in class. Regular effort was also made by the teacher to tell Jim he was OK; for example wishing him a good morning.
- Use open questions – it took a lot of effort but engaging Jim in problem solving eventually came when he went with the class on a geography field trip. He showed a completely different side to his problem-solving abilities. The group was set some initiative tests that revolved around open questions. Jim really got involved and enjoyed the challenge and the success.
- Help him develop leadership roles – Jim was chosen as part of a group to help teach younger children football skills and coach them.
- Give him responsibility – Jim has been helping younger children with their literacy by hearing them read. He has done well; however he has needed some help in remembering to go to sessions. (Start small and don't give up at the first failure.)
- Listen to him – Jim's dad races pigeons. He has got a pigeon called Archie.
- Encourage him to think when asking questions of him – Jim is writing a diary

> to try to work out why he concentrates better during some parts of the day than others. He is going to keep a log of what he eats as well as what he does.
> - Use time to reflect and repair – time out to think about how he is going to make good can be effective after Jim has had a confrontation.
> - Mentor him – show him Adult egostate, so that although Jim finds it hard when he is not shouted at for his behaviour difficulties, he has the opportunity to talk about this and learn different responses.

Some of the most effective learning in school can be found on occasions when pupils make mistakes. In orienteering or any basic map work a teacher chooses a safe area to ensure pupils cannot get into any danger. Getting lost is part of the process of learning to map read. Instructions and information are given to help, but they need to take risks and make mistakes to really learn effectively. The information and instructions comes from Parent but the testing out and experimenting comes from the Adult.

Linking egostates with learning

A healthy school demonstrates all egostates and positive modes at personal and organisational levels and gives its pupils time to explore and refine each for themselves. However it will also be a school that recognises the areas that its pupils need to develop and so has lots of opportunity for practising, in Jim's case Adult transactions (for further discussion see Chapter 6).

Just because teachers, classroom assistants and other adults in school are in a position of responsibility through *loco parentis* it does not mean that they have to operate only from Parent. Often responsibility for safety and well-being is confused with control and power.

In the diagram (Figure 2.7), from an organisational model by Crespelle (1989), the diamonds represent the roles we may be in; teachers will, by definition, be in the higher role in the classroom – they have the responsibility to structure the environment and keep it safe, and to give instruction. The class is in the lower role – the pupils are recipients of teaching and have the right to be protected and instructed. In the staffroom a group of teachers talking together will all be in equal roles. None of these roles prevent us from using all available egostates. A teacher, while in the 'higher' role can employ their Parent knowledge and experience, their Adult reality checking and their Child creativity, and can structure, nurture, take account, be cooperative and spontaneous – as can the pupils while in 'lower' role!

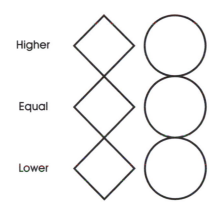

Figure 2.7 Roles (Crespelle 1989)

The secret to resolving conflict is to change what we do! This is when you will notice a change in the conflict; when someone shifts.

- This means you need to cross the transaction and invite a different response.
- You need to remember to address the other person from a positive and not a negative position.

The following is an example which starts with a negative transaction between Parent and Child, i.e. a conflict or the start of one:

Teacher: 'Sarah will you stop talking, you're always talking in my lessons and I'm fed up with it' – Critical Parent.

Sarah ignores the teacher and carries on talking – Rebel Child.

Teacher makes a loud chicken noise. The class laugh, as do the teacher and Sarah. The lesson continues – Natural Child.

The solution is to change from a negative to a positive mode, or to another egostate. If however you opt for a negative mode of another egostate you may stop the communication. If in the process you put down – or in TA terms, *discount* – the other person, then you will store up trouble for yourself later, or even there and then when the discount is returned. Sarcasm would be a good example of this, or embarrassing a pupil in front of the whole class. Teachers and other adults in school should never underestimate the influence they have on pupils even if it is not apparent at the time. The use of put downs, sarcasm and discounts leads to conflict and will ultimately get in the way of a student learning. A discount will serve to lower an individual's self-esteem and make them less able to take risks in relationships and learning. Crossing a transaction positively can transform communication; crossing it negatively prevents real communication until something else changes and it can start again.

The Drama and Winners Triangles

Another way to reduce conflict is to recognise the negative invitation and avoid falling into the trap.

When you find yourself in a situation that is familiar, and uncomfortable, and feels like 'I've been here before' or 'why does this always happen to me', this could be called, in TA terms, a game.

A game is a series of transactions that has a negative pay-off and leaves everyone concerned with a bad feeling. Games are patterns of behaviour that we slot into easily, having learned them early and continued to play them out as familiar ways of relating to others, even though we don't always like the results. Games do not come from the Adult and they are often played out again and again by the same players with the same consequences.

As an illustration, and a way of understanding games, let's look at Karpman's Drama Triangle (1968). This is a way of analysing psychological games as in a thriller.

There are three roles:

- A Victim – 'I'm being hard done to and I'm helpless to change it'
- A Rescuer – 'I'm only trying to help and sort out the problem for you'
- A Persecutor – 'You should do it my way then everything will be alright'

These are shown in Figure 2.8.

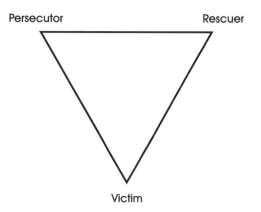

Figure 2.8 The Drama Triangle

Looking at the cartoon (Figures 2.1 and 2.6) you may have thought that both pupil and teacher had unspoken agendas behind their words. These ulterior messages determine the outcome of the transaction – the particular negative stroke that each person ends up with, the 'payoff' of the game. We often pick up these unvoiced messages – the pupil probably has a very good idea about her teacher's motivation in sending for the deputy head. Players may take on one role in the game, and then switch to another role as the game proceeds. This pupil may start out as Victim but she soon switches to Persecuting the teacher, and the teacher struggles to Persecute her back by bringing in a bigger Persecutor who will also be Rescuing the teacher!

Case study

In school the same pupil is sent out of the same class every week. He is sent to a senior teacher. Every week they have a chat and a biscuit and the pupil goes to his next lesson. Nothing ever changes. The same behaviour occurs to get sent out each week. The teacher complains to anyone who will listen about the lack of support you get in school for dealing with pupils with behaviour difficulties. The senior member of staff feels sorry for the pupil each week, and knows that he has probably been misbehaving again. But he has a tough home life and anyway that particular teacher is always sending pupils out, so obviously has no control. No one is happy with the situation. The pupil misses his lesson, the senior teacher can't get on with all the paperwork and the teacher feels unsupported and undervalued. The class teacher appears to Persecute the pupil, and then acts as Victim inviting Rescue by the senior teacher, and also by colleagues. The senior teacher Rescues the pupil and the class teacher, then feels Victim because she can't get her own work done, and may Persecute the class teacher in private or in the staffroom. The pupil seems to be Victim in class but in fact could be seen as Persecutor to the class teacher, while playing the Victim role with the senior teacher. The drama triangle roles swap around. Nobody wins (see Figures 2.9 and 2.10).

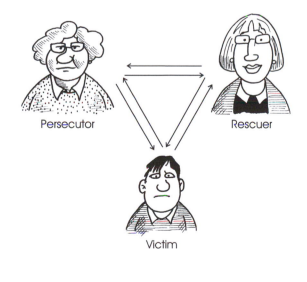

Figure 2.9

How can the roles become more effective? Each of the drama triangle roles has a valid aspect: the Victim has a problem that needs to be solved, the Rescuer feels a real concern for others and the Persecutor wants to put limits on what is expected of them (Choy 1990). To make these real in a positive way new strategies are required:

Persecutor

Rescuer

Victim

Figure 2.10

- The Victim needs to voice feelings – talk to the other game players honestly. And start to problem solve – teacher, pupil and senior need to talk about how they are feeling.
- The Persecutor needs to become proactive and start to define boundaries. Then build up other game players by focusing on what they are good at and times that they have successfully dealt with that particular situation.
- The Rescuer needs to become responsible and support others in doing what they need to and stop doing things for others.

The senior teacher needs to offer time and support to both teacher and pupil at an agreed time, and to also leave time for doing the paperwork. If she cannot offer all the support that is needed then she should find someone who can. However she needs to be sure that the other game players are doing all that they can do to resolve the situation before she steps in. The senior will have established that certain steps have been followed or taken by the teacher before the pupil exits the classroom. The consequence needs to be linked to the behaviour and to have the desired effect, i.e. to stop the behaviour causing the concern.

All the players need to start afresh contracting with each other about what they want and need from each other at appropriate times, with time to review arrangements.

The (positive) paradox is that on the Winners Triangle we can be proactive and responsible, and voice our feelings – all at the same time! This version of the triangle (Figure 2.11) is from Napper and Newton (2000).

Games often lead to or involve conflict, wasting time and emotional energy. They are habitual, sometimes difficult to detect and realise we are in them, and they will always leave us with a negative feeling. Often we are only aware that we have been involved in a game when we have come away from it feeling 'got at' or 'caught out'. However, that is the time to use the drama triangle to work out what role we had and then consider what could be tried next time to take on a winners role. Karpman suggests that each drama triangle role is '10% OK'. We start out with a good intention – to deal with a problem, to offer help, to say what we can or can't do – then something goes wrong because we lack the strategies that will carry out our aim. Thinking about how we can change what we do in conflict situations begins the process of practising different options.

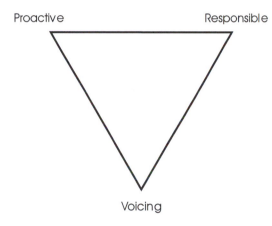

Figure 2.11 The Winners Triangle

Games are ways in which we may have become used to getting recognition for ourselves. Conflict is a negative experience for all concerned. Those best at conflict are often the people we need to engage with the most in our teaching. Reflecting on conflict and how it is engaged in will help develop more productive ways of communicating with people that are more effective and positive for everyone. Picture the classroom after the conflict that was described earlier in the cartoon. The pupil has left, but what sort of lesson will that class and teacher have now? The saying 'You have to lose a battle to win the war', is somewhat misplaced; substitute 'choose your battles and remember which war it was you were supposed to be fighting'. 'Ah yes, my objective was to teach English, not win a conflict with one pupil.' We often lose sight of our main goals – in order to prevent this we need to revisit our purpose regularly.

CHAPTER 3

Partnership Planning: Contracting in School

- Have you ever wondered why partnerships at work go wrong?
- Have you ever thought that you have been working at odds with colleagues?
- Have you ever wondered why sometimes dealing with behaviour can feel like a battle between teacher and pupils?

This chapter explores how TA ideas can impact on contracting in the school context. We raise a number of issues about the limitations of conventional contracting arrangements and offer possibilities for establishing effective relationships between staff and pupils. In many respects the process of contracting is absolutely fundamental to successfully using other TA concepts. No contract – no TA.

Readers may be familiar with the concept of formal contracting; behaviour contracts have been used by teachers for working with individual pupils causing concern for many years. Home–school contracts have also been in operation since the early 1990s and are now required to be in place at the outset of a child's placement at school. The rationale in both instances has been to make clear expectations on each party with an emphasis on preventing further difficulty.

Perhaps the most common form of contract in school is that between a teacher and a pupil whose behaviour has been difficult. Initial, low-key strategies have failed and the teacher considers a more explicit approach is needed, possibly in discussion with a pastoral manager or SENCO. In secondary schools the pupil may be 'on report' or, as is the case in many primary schools, 'put on a programme' as part of an Individual Education Plan (IEP). In both cases the 'contract' is a tool through which the school can both encourage the pupil to recognise appropriate behaviour and identify situations where difficulty continues.

Likewise, establishing the home–school contract enables schools to set out their expectations of parents in terms of pupil behaviour. In some cases this includes a full summary of what the parent and pupil can expect from the school in terms of teaching and learning. In many instances home–school contracting is a mechanism for safeguarding a school's position when difficulties emerge over the management of behaviour, and to a lesser extent non-attendance. This tendency very much reflects the roots of the home–school agreement process; politicians recently have been keen to support head teachers in responding to especially difficult situations with parents. However, as we consider contracting from a TA perspective these 'contracts' might be more appropriately regarded as simply lists of terms and conditions.

Why do we have a contract? Do we need one? Identifying the importance of purpose, outcomes and agendas in contracting

Contracting in schools has been almost entirely associated with things being done to another party, often with a superficial degree of negotiation and rarely within a holistic understanding of the rationale for the contract or its context. Other frustrations that are frequently heard that can be associated with the limitations of conventional contracts include:

- 'This pupil is really beyond the limits – s/he has forgotten/defaced/ripped up their report card for the third time.'
- 'The trouble with families around here is that they place little value on education.'

These are other comments made that indicate limitations of less explicit contracting systems in schools:

- 'The learning support assistant (LSA) in my class doesn't really help at all. S/he undermines what I am trying to do with a pupil/group.'
- 'It's basically a personality clash between that member of staff and the pupil/class/member of staff.'
- 'We, the SEN department, don't 'do' behaviour – that's for heads of year.'
- 'As the LSA in the class I can say that the teacher leaves me to deal with all the problems with the pupil/group.'
- 'This class, they just make me feel that it's me against them.'
- 'The trouble in this school is that behaviour issues always fall to the pastoral team yet we know that the curriculum needs sorting out.'
- 'We wanted the Learning Support Unit to be a resource for staff, but we just don't have the time with all the referrals we have been getting.'

From a TA perspective, contracting not only operates at an explicit, formal level but can be used to understand what is going on under the surface of working practices. For instance, the focus of most behavioural contracts tends to centre on the expectations of the pupil by the teacher – it is understood as a two-way contract. This type of contract is likely to have significant limitations; effective contracting is seldom expressed in two dimensions. In the example of a behaviour contract, both teacher and pupil are subject to expectations made by the school (see Figure 3.1). Any contracting negotiations that do not make explicit reference to the respective expectations on each of the parties are bound to fail. The reason is simple enough: the expectations of the third party – in this case the school – are more often than not the driving force behind the parties having a contract. It is really important to see who is pulling strings behind the scenes. Pupils are often unaware of the school's expectations of the teacher to deliver a specific curriculum, maintain order and discipline, abide by health and safety regulations and other requirements set by the school.

Let's look at an example in more detail. A Year 1 teacher is concerned about a

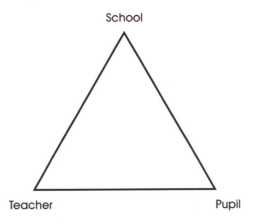

Figure 3.1 A three-cornered contract

pupil who seems to constantly wander round the class avoiding work, chatters through the literacy hour and disturbs others in circle time. The teacher is experienced and has tried a range of low-level techniques – rule reinforcement, differentiated tasks, changed seating plan etc. However, the difficulties persist and the teacher moves ahead with negotiating a typical behaviour contract.

It is crucial for the teacher to address a number of factors in building a deal that (a) will be sustainable and (b) is based on a win–win outcome. Before any discussion takes place about the contract between teacher and pupil, it is imperative that each party shares their relationship within the context of the school. In many respects, it is the combination of the demands of being within the school that underlie the teacher's concerns about the behaviour. The requirement to implement the school's literacy strategy, the drive to raise achievement and the general expectation to have an orderly class are the prime motivators for the teacher's concerns, each of which are rooted in working at that specific school. The *purpose* of the contract is inextricably linked to its context.

The pupil will also have views of what the school expects, not only in terms of her behaviour but also in a more general sense of the purpose of being at school. It is vital to establish what these expectations are at the outset of negotiation, the reason being that both parties need to check out possible misunderstandings – fantasies – about the pressures and agendas that drive each other regarding why the contract is needed.

Clarifying the purpose of the contract is one of a series of principles that can inform effective contracts. For work in schools it is one that can easily be overlooked. In the rush to secure details about who is going to do what, partners can make assumptions about reasons for the work and possibly hold significant misunderstandings about the role of others involved. Table 3.1 illustrates some examples of activities, the purpose driving the work and possible misunderstandings, or fantasies, that might exist.

Activity	Purpose	Fantasies
Group work for disaffected boys at KS4	The group have been identified as most at risk of exclusion by pastoral team – the group work is intended to provide support to sustain their placements	• The boys believe that they are continually being picked on by staff • The boys understand that they are 'special', in preference to disaffected female pupils • Staff are resentful that pupils are being rewarded for poor behaviour
Deploying additional support staff into a Yr 2 class	The class teacher has been identified as having difficulties in planning and delivery of core subject material. Several pupils are now falling behind	• The class teacher believes that senior managers have now acknowledged that s/he has a very difficult class in terms of behaviour • The class teacher believes that his/her lessons have been chosen to give the support assistant an opportunity to practise skills • The assistant understands that the pupils s/he is working with have special educational needs
Developing a home–school agreement with regard to an individual pupil	The school is finding the pupil's behaviour difficult and believes that having parents as allies will help minimise problems	• The parents believe the school is blaming them for their child's behaviour • The child believes all adults pick on him/her

Table 3.1

Linked to the task of clarifying the purpose for the contract is the business of agreeing what the parties want as a result of the contracted activity. Skipping the discussion about purpose can result in a divergent notion of success for each partner. For instance, if an assistant is being deployed into a class for particular sessions it is crucial for the class teacher, assistant and pupils to be clear whether the assistant is to:

- generally support the teacher in the lesson
- work with a specific group of pupils
- work with any pupil.

Only after having clarified this aspect can colleagues then begin to identify whether this activity is likely to have been successful. If the assistant's role is to provide general support to the teacher this might be measured in terms of the teacher's perceptions, e.g. having more time to work directly with all pupils; teaching specific material to those pupils with special needs and those most able; assisting pupils to complete their work and prepare for presentation etc. If the role of the assistant is more specifically targeted at a group of pupils, success may look different and have greater emphasis on individual progress and increased confidence of pupils.

Contracting in schools can sometimes focus too much on describing what partners *must do* and too little on what parties *want to achieve* through working together. In some instances – particularly regarding the provision of additional support, either via internal arrangements or external agencies – there can be an unhelpful preoccupation with *input*. Effective contracting involves 'front-loading' discussions with reference to anticipated outcomes.

One of the possible difficulties that can emerge in contracting in schools is a sense of unease in colleagues exploring the wider context in which the contracted activity is taking place. For example, periods before and after Office for Standards in Education (OFSTED) inspections can raise a number of issues for schools, resulting in a re-prioritising of tasks. Sometimes this leads to making changes in the role of staff or developing specific activities, for example a reorganisation of middle management, establishing an anti-bullying policy or introducing circle time. It might also involve targeting groups of pupils or members of staff where much-needed development work is initiated. In all of these cases it would be necessary to expose the pre-/post-inspection action plan as the driver for the work. Failing to do so can leave colleagues and pupils at liberty to fantasise about the purpose. Some questions worth asking at this stage include:

- Why is this work being developed now?
- How will we know if this has been successful?
- Who wants this work to happen?

Presenting the impact of a third party can be a highly useful mechanism for de-personalising contractual situations. This process is referred to as *three-cornered contracting* or *triangular contracting* (English 1975), although often fourth and fifth parties can also be identified. There is a range of triangular contracts that impact on the work of schools, some of which are presented in Figure 3.2. By exposing the influence of what might be referred to as a 'big power' – which is

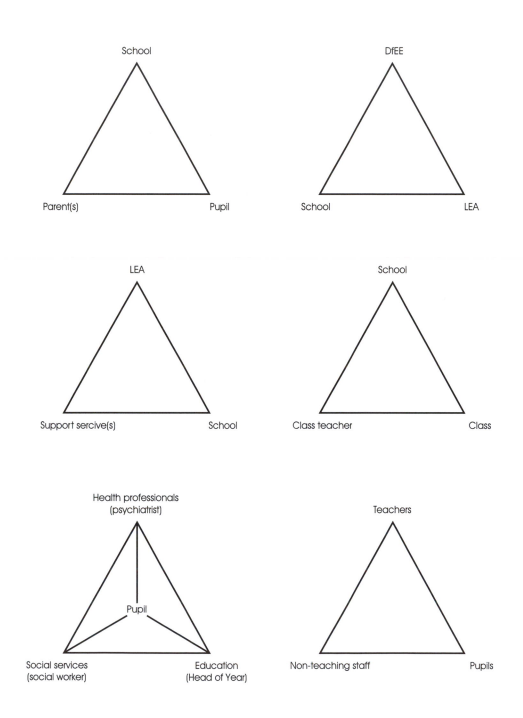

Figure 3.2 Examples of three-cornered contracts

rarely physically present during contracting negotiations – the parties can have more realistic hopes of establishing a sound contract. In effect this stage of contracting enables exposing powerful agendas with a view to setting up transparent arrangements for partners to work together.

In an ideal negotiation representatives from all parties should be present in order to contribute their respective expectations in terms of purpose and anticipated outcomes. However, this is often difficult to arrange, especially given the time constraints that many colleagues in schools have. Sometimes this can be overcome through a 'proxy representative', for example where the position of the head teacher is relayed via the SENCO in a negotiation about support for particular children. It is important to recognise that whenever a third party is absent, the possibility for misunderstanding is greater. This has particular implications for managers in terms of their feeling hijacked or misunderstood when a new project is not going in the direction they had intended. For complex pieces of work, e.g. policy development, targeted groupwork, interventions with other schools/agencies, it is advisable not to initiate project delivery until the lines of communication – including the deployment of any proxy representation – have been fully explored.

Three-cornered contracting is a concept that can be applied to a range of situations in which people will be working together. It might be a one-off training exercise, a specific time-limited project or a long-term working arrangement; in all cases the contracting principles remain the same. This approach to negotiating roles and responsibilities reflects 'Adult behaviour' as discussed in the previous chapter. It is also a deliberate strategy to avoid misunderstandings and minimise 'game-playing' or 'drama triangle' situations, concepts also discussed in Chapter 2.

'Which room have I got?' The importance of domestic details in contracting

Readers may have experienced arriving to deliver a session only to find that the door to the room is locked. Furthermore, the member of staff who has the key – and apparently there is only one copy – is on a course for the day! Or it might be that two colleagues have arranged to team-teach a lesson but each assumed the other was preparing the copying of resources for the pupils. In either case the work planned can be seriously undermined by the oversight.

In negotiating with colleagues we can so easily forget the significance of *procedural* aspects – the contractual domestics. Often this might be due to the familiarity partners have in working together or perhaps to the rushed planning discussions that focused too much on describing what appeared to be more important themes, e.g. which topic to cover or how to identify specific pupils. Some procedural questions might be:

- Where will the work take place?
- When will the work take place? How often?
- What room/equipment/resources/copying will be needed? Who will ensure that these are gathered?
- Are there any funding implications for this work? Who will fund the activity?

In some instances misunderstandings regarding procedural details can be swiftly resolved. However, it is important to recognise that forgetting the apparent peripheral matters of partnership working can send out some very powerful negative messages. This is invariably the case where there have been difficulties in agreeing the purpose for the activity or where there is a history of difficulty in previous work between the parties. Consider the following scenario.

A primary school SENCO and Key Stage 3 coordinator agree that a group of Year 6 pupils need some intensive preparation prior to transition. Relationships with the main feeder secondary school have been patchy in the past but there has been a recent effort to rebuild links, involving a new Head of Year 7 in the secondary school. However, one of the concerns of primary staff is that secondary colleagues ignore information about pupils' primary experience, preferring their own induction assessment system. The negotiations around the work are surprisingly trouble-free and joint work with pupils begins in earnest. However, for the second session there are difficulties as the Head of Year 7 forgot to book a meeting room and much of the meeting time is spent by the group wandering around to find an appropriate place to meet. Staff from the primary school are both disappointed and angry.

In this example the procedural issues around attendance are as important as any other aspect of the contract. The forgetfulness on the part of the Head of Year 7 begins to fuel latent concerns of primary colleagues that the secondary school does not value the transition work. There are a number of consequences, one of which will be a greater degree of suspicion in any future planning between the schools. In drafting effective contracts colleagues ignore the procedural details at their peril!

Horses for courses: defining competency in contracting negotiations

For many colleagues working in schools it can be difficult to say no to requests for help, advice or support. Often this is an important dimension to generating collaborative teams, good relationships in the classroom and efficient systems. In relation to contracting with colleagues, there are some specific aspects that challenge whether it is always helpful to say yes.

One of the reasons why partnerships break down is that partners gradually realise in the delivery of the activity that the expertise required lies outside of the competency of one or both partners. An example of this might be where a classroom assistant is contracted by the SENCO to work with a Year 9 pupil to support literacy skills. The class teacher becomes exasperated that the assistant also has literacy needs and is not able to work effectively. Similarly, it is assumed by the school's behaviour coordinator that an experienced head of department has a ready working knowledge about behaviour theory and then becomes annoyed at recurrent difficulties regarding classroom management.

In both of these cases there may well have been agreement at the contract stage regarding the purpose of the activity, its wider context and procedural aspects. Assumptions were made about the ability of each partner to deliver the contract and therefore problems were likely to emerge. When asking questions about competency a high degree of tactfulness is required. Some questions worth asking to check out professional competency include:

- What expertise does the partner bring to the task?
- How familiar are they with the context in which the work will take place?
- What joint experience do we bring to this task?
- Have the partners worked on similar activities?

There will be many partnership arrangements where the clarification of competency is not a significant issue. Activities where colleagues have been working well together may be safe in their assumptions about respective expertise. Where tasks demand non-specialist skills only a minimal level of clarification may be required. But if this is not the case more explicit clarification is worth pursuing. For instance, if external agencies are engaged in a school-based task it would be appropriate for school staff to reassure themselves that colleagues are competent – not just in terms of carrying out the task itself, but also in understanding school protocols and approach. Similarly, colleagues from the external agency may need to consider whether the demands of the project regarding time commitment, current skill level and awareness of school staff are sufficient to carry out the work.

The competency – in TA contracting terms the *professional* – and procedural dimensions are intended to provide all contracted parties with a degree of *protection*. They are details established at the outset to reassure colleagues and pupils. Neither party should find themselves in a position where they feel vulnerable (due to being asked to do things that they cannot do) or become angry (because basic arrangements have been forgotten that undermine the purpose of the work). An example of this might be where a newly qualified teacher (NQT) is timetabled to teach a group with long-standing and complex needs. While this might provide more experienced colleagues with a break, this in effect sets up both the NQT and pupils to fail – not enough consideration has been given to protect the partners by the 'big powers'.

Process, process, process

Inevitably contracting discussions tend to centre on the business of how colleagues intend to work together – the *process*. As has been commented on earlier, schools sometimes focus too much on this aspect of contracting, and, indeed, it is an important dimension. This area should be addressed having already established the context of the work and its driving forces. Defining roles and responsibilities provides a more detailed picture of what project delivery will look like. It is the part of negotiation that enables colleagues to say what it is they will do and define what they will *not* be doing. It also allows for a more comprehensive discussion of procedural detail.

Questions worth asking relating to process aspects might include:

- How will we work together?
- Who will do what?
- Is there clarity over where different responsibilities lie?
- How will differing roles be made clear to other partners?

Providing for the relapse: addressing psychological aspects in contracting

For the most part the experience of contracting will be of players keen to get started on working together to meet a common goal. During negotiations people will often be anxious to ensure that misunderstandings are clarified to avoid bad feelings and wasted time and effort. Colleagues work on an assumption that given thorough planning, there is a greater likelihood of the activities succeeding. However, experience shows that often things go wrong: people fall ill, diaries become crowded, players move on, new parties move in. A number of factors that fall outside the control of the contracted parties can shift the intended direction of work.

In addition, there may be developments at a psychological level operating outside of the consciousness of individual players. These may not be evident at the outset of negotiation, or even during the early stages of activity. However, these psychological factors may become a dominant feature during the development of working together. One way of illustrating this aspect of contracting is to return to the exemplar material in Table 3.1. In each case there are potential fantasies in the minds of individual parties. One of the dangers in developing the activities might be that people begin to behave as if their fantasy about the other's motivation is real. In other words, a teacher begins to project negative messages about exclusion to parents, despite having asserted that s/he wants their child to be at the school.

In effect, what happens is that individual players can find themselves inadvertently sabotaging contract agreements, but this may only be exposed well into the work. By this point partners may be too angry or disappointed to be able to think about the situation in a helpful way. Consequently things get stuck and in some instances work is abandoned due to overwhelming 'personality' clashes.

One of the most overlooked aspects of planning between colleagues in schools is providing for possible relapses. In our enthusiasm for ensuring that a partnership will work, colleagues may be wary of considering how arrangements might be vulnerable to changed circumstances or shifting perceptions of the partners. It may appear a peculiar recommendation, but inviting partners to consider how arrangements might be undermined can prove a valuable part of the contracting exercise.

Take the example of a class teacher using contracting with their class at the outset of the year in establishing a behaviour code. Asking the class the best responses to inappropriate behaviour is a critical part of building an effective approach to maintaining a positive and safe working environment. Likewise, in negotiating the role of a learning mentor it would be appropriate to consider at the outset how to avoid the possibility of colleagues leaving the mentor alone to deal with pupils' difficulties without support. Relapses are entirely normal developments. In many situations they are also predictable: possible changes in staffing, illness, and breakdown in behaviour. In contracting negotiations potential sabotage questions can include:

- How might partners find themselves undermining the contract?
- What could partners find themselves doing that might sabotage the work?
- What's going on that might threaten success?
- What mechanisms do we have for when things seem to be going wrong?

Finally – *physis* (Greek: meaning 'life-force' or growth)

A sixth aspect to consider when contracting is establishing how the planned work fits in with the wider growth of each of the partners, or physis. The motivation of colleagues is greater where an explicit link can be made with the development of the individual or organisation. For example, it might be important to locate the contracted introduction of circle time with a Year 3 class with a broader school-wide initiative to raise self-esteem. Similarly, in improving a child's behaviour at school parents may be more highly motivated if this is linked to having better relationships at home.

In schools there can be a wide range of separately funded programmes involving a wide range of staff. The contracting process can be invaluable for generating discussion about how individual activity interweaves within a programme of projects. Schools are increasingly encouraged to have work endorsed through the school development plan and this is an obvious route for locating contracted work within the growth of the organisation.

Some questions worth asking that encourage reflection of the physis dimension of the contract include:

- How does this work fit in with our work outside of this partnership?
- How will other colleagues understand this activity in relation to what they are doing?
- Are both partners able to identify 'what's in it for them'?

Contracting principles: summary

Schools have always been the forum for complex contractual situations, regardless of whether these are made explicit or remain at a hidden level. Whether partners are teachers, managers, pupils or parents, contracting principles must apply in establishing effective, sustainable and successful relationships. A summary of the principles is presented below (adapted from Hay 1995):

Contracting: Underlying Principles

Contracts may or may not be written down. A verbal contract is still a contract. The main point is that we discuss and agree why we are interacting as we work together. Contracts operate at different levels – all levels need to be clear to avoid unwitting sabotage.

The 6 Contracting Principles

Procedural *– administrative details, such as when colleagues meet, where, how often, who keeps notes, payment procedure and domestic arrangements, e.g. resources, copying, etc.*

Professional *– what do partners offer in terms of their professional role, what is it that colleagues need and is this within collective competency?*

Purpose *– why are the partners coming together, what do colleagues want to achieve, and how will they know when it has been attained?*

Process – *how do partners intend to arrive at their purpose, how will they work together?*

Psychological – *what might occur outside of partners' awareness, how might any of them sabotage the process?*

Physis – *how does the purpose fit within colleagues' overall growth and development – is this an appropriate pathway to pursue with them?*

The 3 Dimensional 'P's

Protection   – **procedural** *establishes clarity and avoids misunderstandings*
               – **professional** *implies delivering within limits of competency*

Permission – **purpose** *emphasises that partners are permitted to achieve*
               – **process** *establishes an agreed style(s) of interaction*

Potency   – **psychological** *dimensions are made explicit*
               – **physis** *acknowledges the wider context in which partners can grow*

Case study

A group of Year 10 boys would hang around together as 15-year-olds often do, and were frequently caught flouting school rules, for example, smoking during breaks. This pattern also repeated itself outside school with the police and public. Most teaching staff found their physical appearance and the language they used very intimidating. The group was also regarded as having racist tendencies after an incident in the canteen when they got into conflict with a group of black boys. The group all had experience of exclusion and were at risk of not being entered for various GCSEs.

The boys had all been 'on report' when they were in Years 8 and 9 for longer than their Head of Year cared to remember. All of the boys felt they had been 'done unto' and believed that the report had little in it for them given that they had not been involved in setting it up. The boys' parents had been called to school, they had numerous exclusions and they had all signed various lists of terms and conditions for re-entry to school following exclusion. The school's frustration at the uselessness of these arrangements was evident.

The group was referred by the school to the local behaviour support service in a last ditch attempt to salvage some value out of the boys' troubled school career. The first task of the support staff was to establish a triangular contract. The contracting process became the core part of the intervention, taking up almost half of the period of support. Sometimes we can underestimate just how

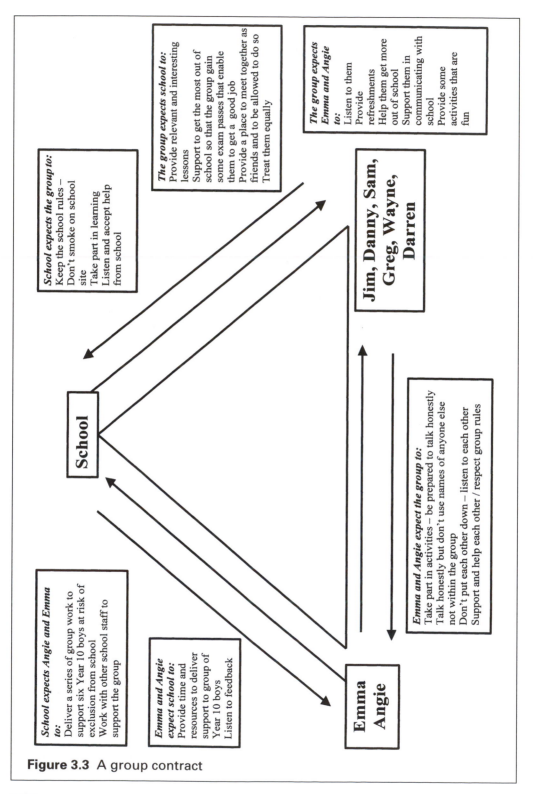

Figure 3.3 A group contract

fundamental contracting principles are to working effectively with one another and the entrenched difficulties that can develop when its principles have been ignored. Equally, while there may be pressure on colleagues to rush initial negotiations it is always worth resisting the urge to leapfrog the process. Partnership planning undoubtedly works, but it takes time.

Contracting became an important activity for the boys. They were focused on the exercise and quickly understood the additional dimensions to talking through a three-cornered contract between themselves, the support service and the school. The summary of their discussions was as follows and a triangular contract for the work is presented in Figure 3.3.

Procedural – Times were set for the group to meet. It was agreed that it could take place in lesson time but not in the same lesson every week and the time would rotate to ensure this. Drinks and biscuits would be provided by the service and a quiet room would be made available in the school with comfortable chairs. The sessions would last for one hour and start and finish with lesson times so no one would be wandering into lessons half-way through. The group would need to enter and leave the room calmly so as not to disrupt other classes.

Professional – The group needed to be prepared to participate. This meant voicing their individual opinions and contributing to discussions. The need for respect for both each other and support staff was also emphasised. A situation developed in the second session that tested this principle. The group arrived in an excitable mood, the boys were noisy and barged into the room knocking things over. This did not go unnoticed by other teachers working nearby and the incident bought into question the competency of the group workers to manage the group. This was discussed with the group who were reminded that any further incidents would jeopardise the continuation of the group. This startled the group and their behaviour on entry and exit for all future sessions was much improved.

The group leaders negotiated to offer the group activities in a time that was considered their own. The sessions provided a level of confidentiality (within the local child protection guidelines, which were explained to the group), and each pupil also agreed to keep the personal contributions of others confidential to the group.

Purpose – The purpose of the group was to support the boys in making best use of their remaining time at the school. The objective was to keep them in school and to provide them with an outlet for their views, feelings and aspirations for the future. It was made clear that this was an agenda set by and between the school and service. The boys in turn were invited to buy into this aim.

Process – The processes of negotiating the contract and running the group were similar, based on mutual respect. It was intended at the outset that the views of the boys would be seriously regarded by the school and this involved members of the school team attending for some sessions. This was an important point – if the boys were being expected to demonstrate a higher level of respect, the school would need to find ways to reciprocate.

Psychological – The group always had the option of regarding the support service staff as part of the establishment – the school – and that consequently they conspired against the boys. The group leaders had to ensure that they did not collude with the teaching staff or the group. By raising this possibility at the outset some of these anxieties were minimised. Similarly, by involving school staff in the sessions, the support staff reassured possible anxieties that they were working in collusion with the group.

Physis – The group wanted and needed to develop the aims of the group. They all shared ambitions and wanted to access college and work. The process of the group aimed to help them take some control of that process. In many respects the purpose of the work reflected another important development for the boys. If we consider the drama triangle positions, the boys made it clear that they saw themselves as being picked on by staff, that they were the victims, whereas staff saw their menace and disruption as persecutory. The intention of the group process was to nurture growth away from these unhelpful positions and move towards a greater level of personal autonomy. The work with the group focused on inviting them to engage in their Adult egostate, while also working with school staff in reducing an over-use of Critical Parent behaviour.

The group sessions had a number of outcomes. The boys produced a formal document for school staff explaining how they perceived their experience. This included, for example, reference to their congregation as a group as the time when they felt they could be heard or felt safe. The incident that led to teaching staff identifying the group as racist was also explored. The group maintained that the conflict had been started by the other group and this led to a whole series of sessions on defining racism. This resulted in the group being able to feedback to the school on the incident using Adult egostate, in preference to the previous Adapted Child response. The group report also included a completed copy of the contract and was presented to the head teacher and other staff in school. The sessions had started the process for the boys in working with the school in a different way and enabled them to take greater control of their school careers.

None of the group was excluded from school and all completed their GCSEs.

Moving to a partnership planning model

Having a written contract is a common expectation when working in partnerships. In schools there is a range of systems that might be described as including possible contracts:

- Individual Education Plans
- Statements of Special Educational Needs
- Pastoral Support Plans
- Service level agreements between schools and services

All of these systems have associated administration, invariably involving the completion of differing proformas. We have been developing an approach centred on TA contracting over a number of years in different contexts which we call *partnership planning*. Unlike conventional contract arrangements, partnership planning is a

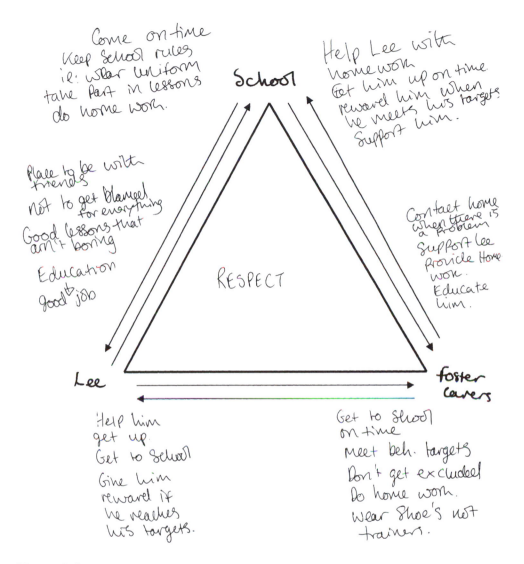

Come on time
Keep School rules
ie: wear uniform
take part in lessons
do home work.

Help Lee with
home work.
Get him up on time.
reward him when
he meets his targets.
Support him.

Place to be with
friends
not to get blamed
for everything
Good lessons that
aren't boring

Education
good job

School

RESPECT

Contact home
when there is
a problem.
Support Lee
Provide Home
work.
Educate
him.

Lee

foster
carers

Help him
get up.
Get to School
Give him
reward if
he reaches
his targets.

Get to School
on time
meet beh. targets
Don't get excluded
Do home work.
wear shoe's not
trainers.

Figure 3.4

highly detailed contract that focuses on a tightly defined task, which could include
any of the situations listed above. Accompanying records of the partnership plan are
more than simply administrative tools. Proformas have been developed that ensure
that the central contracting principles are addressed during negotiations. In other
words, where colleagues use partnership planning proformas they significantly
minimise the potential for frustrated or misunderstood contracts.

Clearly not all contracts are recorded using formal proformas – the teacher
negotiating expectations with her class is unlikely to want to use a proforma. In
these instances a more flexible approach is to use a large, hand-drawn triangle on

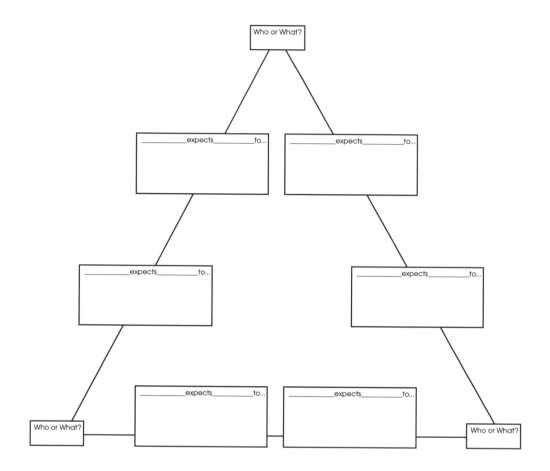

Figure 3.5 Three-cornered contract proforma

which are pegged the expectations of the pupils, school and class teacher along respective sides of the triangle (see Figure 3.4). Where written records are necessary a proforma can be used (see Figure 3.5).

The important point to remember with partnership planning is that the contract is a 'live' document. It is the reference point for the joint task: when there is confusion or lack of clarity on any aspect, the contract serves as agreed statement of intent. It is equally important to recognise that the contract is live in a sense that it can be reviewed and changed at any time. While a date might be set to formally review the work, the contract can be referred to by any party at any time when one group is unhappy with how things are developing.

Specific guidance for using partnership planning

Experience indicates that invariably it takes longer to plan and arrange a project than is anticipated. Although the initial suggestion for a project will lead to swift conclusions as to what the work might look like, it is crucial that the detail of work is considered and this is often complex (see Figure 3.6).

It is expected that the planning will take at least two meetings and, for complex work, will span a period of weeks. The more partners that are involved, the greater the potential for games and consequently the need for more time.

The final draft plan cannot be completed without the direct involvement of the colleagues involved in delivering the work. This can mean drawing in class teachers, assistants, managers or support personnel at the earliest possible stage in planning. The longer these key players are left outside of discussions, the more likely it will be that the initial concept of the project will be misunderstood.

Copies of the final draft need to be copied to all partners, even when these colleagues have been absent from more detailed discussions.

Experience has shown that all sections of planning proformas must be completed prior to starting the project. Each component is designed to minimise the potential for misunderstanding and ambiguity. Attention should be given to the main objectives of the project as opposed to the level of resource required; *outcomes*, not input, should be the overriding concern (which is different from acknowledging the importance of process).

Where a triangular contract is being drawn up with pupils or colleagues, it is crucial that all sides of the contracting dynamic are considered. Ignoring any of the three dimensions leaves a significant weakness in the contract.

Questions to ask to ensure effective partnership planning:

Are there any specific issues to check out regarding the following arrangements:

- Dates and time of activities
- Confidentiality protocols
- Venue
- Payment
- Providing resources
- Staff involved

Is the partnership focused on activity that is within the competency of partners?

Do all players have the potential capability, opportunity and understanding to fully participate in the activity?

Do all parties have a clear understanding of the purpose of the work?

How will each partner know that the activity has been successful?

(Continued)

How will the partners work together?

Are all players aware of their specific responsibilities with the plan of work?

What might each partner do that could undermine the partnership?

How might difficulties be either avoided or addressed when they emerge?

How does the activity integrate with the overall development of each partner and the school as an organisation?

Figure 3.6 Partnership planning checklist

CHAPTER 4

Raising Self-Esteem

- Do you sometimes wonder why a pupil doesn't respond well to praise?
- What are the links between self-esteem and learning?
- What are the links between self-esteem and teaching?

In this chapter we will consider how recognition and affirmation can affect motivation and self-esteem, using the TA concepts of strokes, life positions and script. Strokes, defined as units of recognition, were described by Berne as a human need or 'hunger' without which we cannot thrive. The decisions we make, based on our early experience, and our consequent behaviour are all designed to ensure that we get strokes from the other people in our world.

Maggie's day

The alarm went as usual at 6.45 a.m. but Maggie had gone to bed so late the night before after finishing the marking that she only half heard it and surfaced 10 minutes later when it sounded for the third time. Struggling with tiredness she got out of bed leaving Chris still sleeping and staggered into the kitchen to put the kettle on. The washing-up had been done, the kitchen was tidy. Amazing! Someone had wanted to help, and even in her half-conscious state Maggie felt more cheerful. But she must hurry if she was to be in time to get the classroom ready as she had planned for today's lessons. Tea – better. Toast – even better, especially as the kitchen genie seemed to have cleaned the crumbs out of the toaster. Shower – someone had used the last of her shower gel. Grrr! Mug of tea for Chris. 'Thanks love, see you tonight.' Oh well. Freezing cold outside, forgotten her gloves, no time to go back. Will the car start? No? Yes! Maybe I'll make it after all. Anxious, impatient, cursing slower drivers, Maggie arrived only a few minutes later than she'd hoped at the school. Children already hanging around in groups, in their own world until the battle of the school day started at 8.50 a.m. A few said 'hello, miss', more dispiriting surly looks, then two boys called a friendly greeting. As Maggie approached they began talking to her about the pigeons that hung around the school playground. Most of the boys just saw the pigeons as 'flying

---

rats' but these two had noticed the differences in appearance and behaviour in the birds and had given names to some of them, which they wanted to tell her. Strangely buoyed up by this exchange, and the knowledge that the boys had realised she would be interested and not laugh at them or tell them off, Maggie hurried to the staffroom. Disaster. As soon as she saw Andy she knew what was about to happen.

Andy asked if Maggie had received his memo in her pigeon-hole about OFSTED. Before she could answer 'no' he asked her for the updated plans by Friday, if not before, and by the way had she got copies of her department's 'inclusion policy'; he needed that for Friday too. Then he strode off to catch someone else. Maggie had hardly caught her breath. Her heart sank; she had spent ages compiling the plans she had already given him. Not even any recognition of the work she had already done – and 'inclusion policy', what 'inclusion policy'?

As Maggie went to her first class she felt the good feeling she had after the 'pigeon' incident fade away. Why was Andy so abrasive, and why didn't he listen to what she said? The class were their usual ebullient selves, but this time she couldn't cope with their noise and energy and set them an unwelcome task that caused resentful looks and muttered complaints. So much for her fabled ability to get on with difficult pupils.

Let's run that one again.

Andy walked over to Maggie. He smiled. 'Well done, I've just seen your end of module results,' he said. 'It's great, I mean that, even though now I'm about to ask you a favour. You know Jen is off, well she has got 4w this afternoon and I have

got supply cover, but I wondered if you'd take them as you know them. You know what they're like, they'll rip a supply to shreds. Please?' Maggie pulled a face. 'What's it worth?' she smiled. 'How about the knowledge that the kids will have a good lesson with you there?' 'OK, flattery will get you everywhere, but you've got to give me more time to do my inclusion policy as you're using up all my non-

contact time.' 'OK it's a deal, thanks you saved my life, I'll buy you a pint on Friday.' Maggie smiled as she hurried to her first class, ready to cope with 3f's usual exuberance. All morning the kids seemed really engaged in their tasks, including those who often presented difficulties.

Understanding Maggie's day

Each of the two case study scenarios is a potential everyday experience in school. The ideas in the next few pages will explore how and why we react the way we do to different triggers.

We all need to know we matter. We are constantly interpreting the way other people react to us and interact with us – sometimes we do this consciously and sometimes not. Maggie's day, up to her encounter with Andy, was fairly balanced – some negative experiences (oversleeping, surly looks), some positive (the tidied kitchen, the pigeon incident), and some were neutral and open to different interpretations or perceptions. So she was ready for the day to be a good one.

But added to these everyday happenings are the background tensions that Maggie carries, along with many other teachers. Increasing workload, ever-changing administrative duties, National Curriculum requirements, impending OFSTED inspection, low morale – an endless list of stress-inducing demands that can lead to despair and burn-out. As if this wasn't enough for Maggie to cope with, there are also difficult working relationships to contend with: unreasonable management, colleagues who don't pull their weight, simple personality clashes and differences of values or vision. Why does anybody do it? Well, there are some clues in Maggie's day: real contact with pupils, an affirming request from Andy, plus a personal and corporate sense of achievement when things go well and a desire to educate in the true sense in spite of difficulties – a love of teaching. Recognition for who you are and what you do.

Introducing strokes

The TA term for recognition is 'strokes'; a single stroke is a 'unit of recognition'. A stroke can be:

- verbal – 'How are you today?' 'I don't want to talk to you'
- non-verbal – a smile, a frown
- written – a report, a complaining letter

It may be delivered through:

- sight – a piece of work put on the wall, or not
- hearing – praise, criticism
- touch – a hug, a push
- taste – a favourite meal
- smell – a pleasant scent.

It can be for:

- who we are – 'I really like you', 'you irritate me', or
- what we do – 'this is good work', 'this is full of mistakes, do it again'.

And, most importantly, it can be:

- positive, inviting us to feel OK about ourselves, other people and the world, or
- negative, inviting us to feel not-OK about ourselves and/or others and/or the world.

We all need to know we are valued, that others notice us and care about what we do, that we are part of the human race. This recognition is a biological need, like food; without it we fail to flourish. Strokes are nourishing, life-giving and life-enhancing. And here is a paradox: because strokes are so important to us, we would rather have negative strokes than none at all, just as we would rather eat unsuitable or tasteless food than go hungry. Here's how it happens.

Creating our life-script

When we are small we adapt to the people around us, who protect and nurture us, and have power over us, in ways that will get us the acceptance, approval and acknowledgement we crave. We receive and process information constantly about who we are; how others see us; who or what we are like; what the big people predict for us; what happens to people like us; what the norms, expectations and precedents are in our family. This information comes through what we hear from our care-givers and others, what we observe happening in our world, and through stories, television, films and videos which offer us a range of characters to choose from in our attempt to answer the question 'What happens to someone like me?' And we create out of all this, with our inadequate knowledge and immature thinking, our own personal life-story about who we are and what we will do in the future. This seems to us to be the best way for us to survive and to get the protection and strokes we need. This story, known as 'life-script' or simply 'script', includes beliefs about the world and our place in it, and decisions derived from them. For instance we might come to believe 'People like me never amount to anything' and so decide 'there's no point in trying' or 'You have to work hard to get on' so 'I'll work hard so people will praise me'. These beliefs and decisions will be affected by our culture, family, gender, our place in the family, and by what happens to us. Knowing we are loved or not being sure, big people taking time for us or ignoring us, those around us being kind or cruel or in between, losing or gaining a friend – all these will have an impact on our 'little' thinking. This process is outside our conscious awareness, so as we grow up and act out our beliefs and decisions, we think these are just the way the world is; we remain unaware that we have constructed this 'story' ourselves.

Windows on the world

So we may have decided, overall, that we are 'better' than others; or that others are 'better' than us; or that no one is any good and nor are we; or, hopefully, that on the whole both we and other people are OK; they can be trusted and will like and respect us and we will reciprocate. Most probably it will be a mixture with one attitude dominant; these are known as 'life positions':

- I'm OK, you're not OK
- I'm not OK, you're OK
- I'm not OK and you're not OK either
- and the healthy decision, I'm OK, you're OK.

One of these will be the main theme of our script, and strokes, or the recognition and attention we receive, both help to form our script and determine what sort of strokes we will aim to get. Julie Hay (1993) describes these four positions as 'windows on the world'; each one gives us a different perspective as we look out of that 'window', and we interpret everything that happens to us to fit that perspective.

How would a pupil looking at the world through each of the windows in Figure 4.1:

- respond to praise?
- respond to criticism?
- take part in class/school activities?

Figure 4.1 Windows on the world

What type of strokes would they expect to get/give? with teachers? with other pupils?

Maggie, as we have described her, is probably I'm OK, you're OK most of the time. But if she gets a powerful negative stroke, such as Andy making demands while ignoring what she was saying, she may flip into I'm not OK, you're OK or

I'm not OK and nor are you, and the rest of the school day shows this and affects how she gives and receives strokes in her classes. If she gets a really positive stroke such as Andy's praise of her teaching ability she might stay in a I'm OK, you're OK place all day (give or take a few minor lapses), and again her patterns of stroking in class will reflect this. If she basically feels OK about herself and other people, and is not otherwise stressed out, she will be able to ride a certain amount of negativity from people around her. At the same time every one of her pupils, and every other child in the school, has their own expectations of what strokes they can get – and some of them may already have decided that negatives are all they can get and all they are entitled to.

Why won't some pupils accept praise?

Strokes, and stroke theory, are about much more than positive or negative reinforcement that assumes that all pupils will respond well to rewards. Not so – as many teachers have discovered. If a pupil (or a teacher) has a history of experiencing mostly negatives s/he may be made very uncomfortable by an 'overdose' of positives, and may react in a way that will restore the internal balance. Imagine a seesaw evenly balanced with positives at one end and negatives at the other as in Figure 4.2.

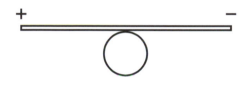

Figure 4.2

The amount and type of strokes which keep the seesaw in balance are, for each of us, our unique personal pattern of the strokes we have learned to expect. Suppose that for Kim, aged eight, every positive leads to an expectation of three negatives –

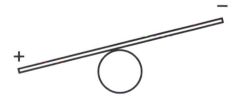

Figure 4.3

the proportion Kim has become accustomed to at home and at school – to maintain the 'mental balance' of the seesaw. A friendly and caring (but maybe not too observant) teacher may offer a large number of positives in a short time for everything done right. The seesaw then looks like this (Figure 4.3).

What does Kim do in order to feel comfortable? Makes sure to get enough negatives to restore the balance – and that will be three times as many as the positives the teacher gave. This is the child that rips up the piece of work for which they have just been praised.

Learning to accept and absorb unfamiliar strokes takes time if it goes against the decisions we made in the early script stage about who we are. Kim's teacher will do better to offer a single, genuine, positive stroke, and be sure that Kim has taken it in before following up with more. Alternatively, the teacher might ask Kim 'How do you want me to let you know when you have done something well?' and let Kim decide on the best level of strokes.

Case study

Danny, a 15-year-old in a unit for excluded pupils, only started to accept strokes when the best stroke was 'that piece of maths is OK' rather than an enthusiastic 'that's brilliant'. When the teacher tried the latter Danny ripped up his work. 'OK' was the highest stroke, given when a very good lesson had been achieved. This started a slow change in the praise Danny could accept. Danny was like a baby as far as accepting strokes went and, like a baby needing milk to drink rather than a steak to eat, he could only accept very small amounts of praise until gradually he acquired the stomach for more.

Why do we do this? As human beings our need for strokes is so great that we will do whatever we need to in order to get them: if acceptance is not offered we will go for approval; if we don't get that we will settle for disapproval; and *in extremis* we will go for outright rejection rather than being ignored. Some examples are: pupils frequently arriving late for lessons, recurrent detentions and the goading of teachers. We also learn very early that some familiar strokes are easy to get – and these may well be the negative ones that tired or irritated parents and teachers hand out, but at least they are acknowledgement that we are there and that's better than nothing. We soon learn to play the psychological games that will guarantee these familiar strokes, and so reinforce our beliefs about ourselves and 'justify' our behaviour, and our thinking and our beliefs about how people see us.

How we discount

Here we need to briefly mention discounts, which will be explored further in the next two chapters. Discounting is the process by which we ignore, disregard or minimise some aspect of ourselves, other people, or the situation. Strictly speaking it is an internal process, which can be inferred by observing a person's behaviour or attitude, but the term has come to be used in a more general way to describe some interactions. Discounting is important in thinking about strokes because:

- Internal discounting of ourselves may result in ignoring or belittling an offered stroke, e.g. 'You did a good job on that report.' 'Oh, it wasn't me I had to ask for help from Head of Year.' With pupils this mechanism may sometimes serve the purpose of defending against unfamiliar and therefore uncomfortable strokes, or it may prevent them from acknowledging progress and positive change. Such discounts, when noticed, can be challenged.
- Discounts may be confused with negative strokes; to see them separately remember that a straight negative stroke will take account of reality, 'You made a lot of mistakes in this work, I don't think you were listening when I told you what to do', whereas a discount will distort reality in some way, 'You never get anything right!'
- All games, and all negative script beliefs and decisions, include discounts; someone's thinking, feelings or intention is not taken account of, and not stroked. We enter games in the hope of getting positive strokes (maybe this time it will work); we don't get them, and settle for the negatives (again). The difference between the drama triangle and the winners triangle is that in the latter transactions are from 'I'm OK, you're OK', resulting in straight and effective strokes, including those times when the aim is to deal with unacceptable behaviour.
- While strokes are life-giving, discounts are life-denying. They show that someone in the transaction is not taking account of something – their own needs, the other person's or the full reality of the situation.

How we can change

The good news is that all self-limiting decisions, and all negative stroking patterns, can be changed! We have constructed them ourselves, and pushed the process and the results out of our awareness. By increasing our awareness and re-deciding our perspectives we can practise new ways of relating to others and so increase our positive stroke quotient, our self-esteem and our sense of purpose and motivation. In doing so we model a different approach for learners and colleagues and even begin the kind of cultural change that will be discussed in Chapter 6.

School can provide a place where pupils can develop new patterns of accepting positive strokes and begin to live out different script decisions based on experience of acceptance as a valued person. This is particularly important in cases where home stroking patterns are mostly negative.

Pupils in school are still in the process of completing their personal scripts. When they are offered information about themselves and their environment which is structured, encouraging, takes account of reality and models cooperation and enthusiasm (in other words, positively stroked from all egostates), they have the opportunity to incorporate this into the dynamic process of script formation and adjust some of the negative decisions they may have made.

Research by Angela Devlin in *Criminal Classes* (1997) asks the question: What was it about those young people who had the same socio-economic backgrounds, negative home circumstances and environments and yet one ended up in prison the other did not? What made a difference? The answer is – a significant adult, often a teacher. At some time there was a person and a place that showed that young person a different way of doing things. This person, when traced, was usually unaware of their role. When told that they had been quoted as that young person's 'significant figure' or ally they were invariably shocked, as they were usually the ones that had kept the pupil at the end of a lesson to talk to. Teachers, because of the way they are often referred to nationally, and because of their workload, sometimes discount the effect and influence that they can have on their pupils. They can and do have an effect every day. That influence in a primary school is over those 30+ pupils in a class, and in a secondary school can be over 180+ pupils a day.

Some things to note about strokes

- Strokes can be positive (inviting us to feel OK) or negative (inviting us to feel not-OK), and unconditional (for being) or conditional (for doing) (Figure 4.4). If we combine the two axes of positive–negative and unconditional–conditional, we get a matrix of acceptance, approval, disapproval and rejection (Temple 1999b).
- We all have our personal preferences and needs for particular strokes: for being intelligent, or attractive, or helpful etc. So we may filter out the ones we don't want or don't recognise. Similarly, we can 'bank' the ones we value, to be drawn on when we need them, if we are feeling stressed or neglected.
- There are some myths around, which are passed on through generations, that strokes are like money – they will run out if spent, they have to be earned, they shouldn't be given away without good reason etc. The *stroke economy*

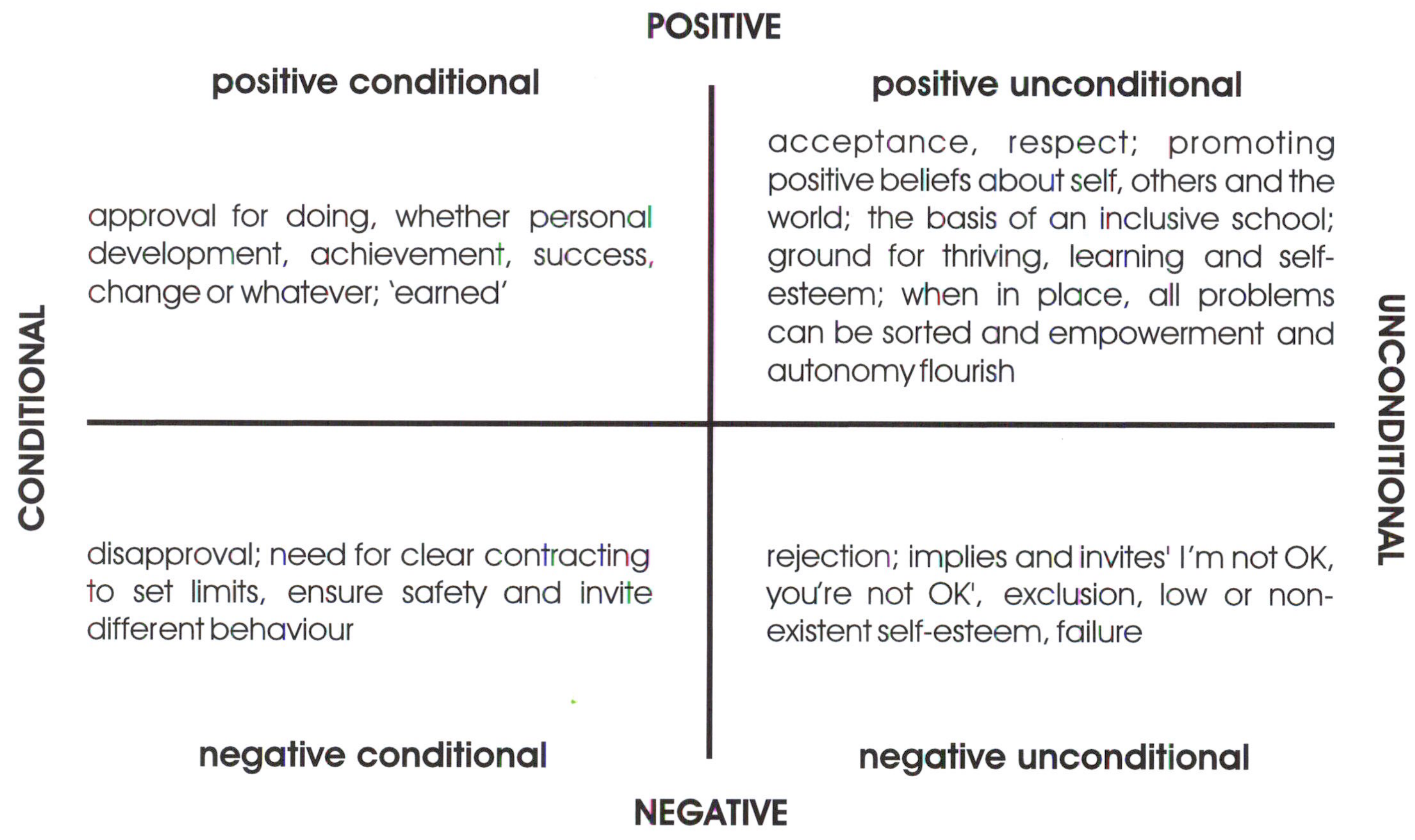

UNCONDITIONAL

POSITIVE

NEGATIVE

positive unconditional

acceptance, respect; promoting positive beliefs about self, others and the world; the basis of an inclusive school; ground for thriving, learning and self-esteem; when in place, all problems can be sorted and empowerment and autonomy flourish

negative unconditional

rejection; implies and invites' I'm not OK, you're not OK', exclusion, low or non-existent self-esteem, failure

positive conditional

approval for doing, whether personal development, achievement, success, change or whatever; 'earned'

negative conditional

disapproval; need for clear contracting to set limits, ensure safety and invite different behaviour

CONDITIONAL

Figure 4.4

rules say ' don't give, ask for or accept strokes, don't reject the ones you don't want, and above all don't give yourself strokes' (Steiner 1971). In fact careful observation tells us that the truth is the opposite – available strokes increase the more they are given, accepted and asked for, and when those not wanted are refused.

- Stroking from an OK–OK position is always positive, even if the information being conveyed is unwelcome, because it shows respect and care and a belief that the other person can do something differently.
- Strokes can be given from and received in any mode; Chapter 6 illustrates this.
- You may have heard of strokes as warm fuzzies (+) and cold pricklies (–). These terms are from the early days of TA, especially from *A Fuzzy Tale* by Claude Steiner (1977). This is a TA fairytale about a time when warm fuzzies were freely available until a wicked witch came along and told everyone that they would run out and that cold pricklies were an acceptable substitute. It is an effective allegory; however, there are also warm pricklies – strokes that start positive and end with a 'sting' ('that's quite good – pity about your awful writing'), and cold fuzzies – jokey or ironic dismissive strokes ('you never get it right, do you?' – said with a smile to show you care really). So we think the straightforward terms more useful.

Using strokes effectively

An understanding of how strokes work, and of the varied needs and reactions of pupils, offers possibilities for a range of alternative strategies for keeping communication clear and raising self-esteem. Here are some ideas:

- Keep it straight and genuine from an 'I'm OK, you're OK' stance. Your colleagues, managers, pupils and pupils' parents may or may not be coming from a similar place; never mind. If you continue to invite them into OK–OK transactions one of two things will happen – either they will respond in kind and communication and self-esteem will improve, or they won't. If that is their choice *you* still save your energy and your own sense of self-esteem by not colluding in negative life positions.
- Observe the needs and reactions of your pupils and colleagues, and note what is effective in promoting positive communication; adjust your comments and feedback to maximise benefit.
- Try a feedback sandwich: preface and follow the straight negative stroke with positives, e.g. 'You have put a lot of work into this and overall it is good. However the spelling and grammar are awful and you need to do something about that. I will spend some time with you looking at specific things that need correcting.'

- Research shows that young people who are attributed with positive and desirable characteristics develop them (Dieser 1997)! For example: 'You are a quiet and task focused class' has much more effect than 'You should be quiet when you are working individually' *or* 'Be quiet – you are too noisy'. Strange but true. Many teachers appear to believe that Critical Parent instruction and negative strokes will eventually be effective. The evidence is that Structuring and Nurturing Parent and Adult positives work better. A quick way of expressing this is 'What you stroke is what you get'. Attention to cooperative behaviour, authentic feelings and individual thinking has much more chance of bringing these about than attention to resistance, rule breaking and mistakes.
- Be aware of cultural differences in stroking patterns – if in doubt, ask a more experienced colleague, or the person themselves (see Jill's story below).
- Kids know plastic strokes (insincere) and marshmallows (too sweet, squishy and not really nourishing) when they hear them. So praise when appropriate, keep a positive atmosphere, and avoid over the top, flippant or automatic strokes which debase the currency.
- Stroke the Rebel Child! It is an attempt to be heard, to say 'I'm here, this is me' or 'I don't like what's going on here – I want something to be different'. Acknowledging the energy and the need can invite a shift into cooperation. 'I know you are angry about what happened just now and I can understand that. What do you need to help you stay here for 10 minutes?'
- Teachers need strokes too! Know your own needs, your sources of positive strokes and the triggers that invite you into a negative position. All teachers want to be valued for their skill, expertise, experience, creativity or whatever.

The following list was drawn up by the staff of one school.
We value being:

- trusted to get on with the job
- respected and not taken for granted
- acknowledged – a word of thanks, a smile, a quick hello
- listened to
- consulted
- appreciated
- respected
- told that we are valued, and are doing a good job
- encouraged by staff outside the immediate working environment
- told about good things we have done
- trusted to do our best both socially and professionally
- thanked verbally for things

and we want to be valued for:

- what we do although it may not seem a lot
- experience and knowledge of early years education
- doing something well – making a positive contribution
- knowledge and experience of working in a variety of schools
- knowledge about teaching and learning
- commitment to the job and to raising pupil achievement
- being honest and open
- hard work and enthusiasm
- expertise in early years and basic skills teaching
- being who we are.

This list, which was drawn up in a way that ensured anonymity so that no individual teacher was linked to any particular stroke, became the basis of a new understanding among the staff and a contract to raise positive stroke levels in school. At a practical level that included, among other things, increasing staff contact time through rearranging breaks, visiting each other's classrooms to appreciate colleagues' work and consulting about proposed changes to timetables.

- Who do you need to ask to acknowledge you and who do you acknowledge? How can you raise the stroke quotient in your school? Sometimes teachers seem to believe that they are *only* OK if their pupils know everything; if their classes are quiet and obedient; or if they are the most innovative and creative teacher in the school (Montuschi 1984); and it has to be said that some school cultures may encourage these ideas. A potentially healthier, and certainly less stressful, approach could be:\teachers are responsible for structuring the learning environment, encouraging pupils, taking account, showing enthusiasm and cooperation; and if that is in place, pupils are responsible for the outcome.\In Chapter 6 we explore how the school ethos can support both pupils and teachers and introduce ways of assessing 'school egostates' and stroke patterns.
- Schools (and some parents and teachers) tend to emphasise conditional strokes – for learning well, keeping the rules, being good at sport, being helpful, achieving things. Fine – we all need approval. More importantly we also need to be accepted.(An atmosphere of acceptance and inclusion, and a belief that everyone is intrinsically OK no matter how not-OK their behaviour may be, can change a school – not to mention the world.)
- What you stroke is what you get. Whatever gets the attention increases which is why some people continue to go for negatives – that was what got the response in the past. So ask yourself: what sort of strokes are available, encouraged or outlawed in your school? How is recognition given? Is it different for different groups? How easy or difficult is it to communicate vertically and laterally?

- Our overall aim is to promote autonomy. Claude Steiner (1974) suggests ten 'rules for raising kids for autonomy' for parents. Based on this, we have created 'ten rules for teaching for autonomy' for teachers, who have a unique opportunity to promote awareness, spontaneity and emotional literacy in learners.

1. Be prepared to extend appropriate nurturing and protection to create a safe space for learning.
2. The principal aim of teaching for autonomy is to provide the learner with freedom to fully exercise their faculties for awareness and spontaneity. No other goal is put above autonomy – not even success, self-control, social adaptation or any other goal desired by teachers – if it contradicts the main goal of autonomy. Autonomy was defined by Berne (1964) as the capacity for *awareness* of self and others, *spontaneity* and *intimacy* – we think *openness* is a better word for the latter. We discuss this further in Chapter 6.
3. Encourage learners to give, ask for, accept and reject strokes, and to brag. Openness is defeated through persistent negative strokes.
4. You can empower learners by affirming their rationality, feelings and intuition. Awareness is defeated through discounts.
5. Explain your reasons for non-negotiable rules; enable negotiation where possible and agree a contract. Spontaneity is defeated by arbitrary rules.
6. Be truthful and honest with learners. If you do not know something say so, and enjoy finding out together.
7. Be potent, responsible and open. When you are assertive, listen actively and share problem solving, you provide OK–OK modelling for learners.
8. Encourage sharing, respect, cooperation and setting of personal goals. This will discourage competition and increase self-esteem.
9. Be responsible for your own feelings and needs.
10. Trust human nature and believe in people.

- Strokes are the way we bond as members of a community, whether a family, a peer group, a school or a society. We can make changes through stroking patterns at macro level by considering the whole school culture and at micro level by altering the style and content of our transactions in the classroom. Sometimes the two will go together; other times we might decide to concentrate on the smaller group as the place where we can be most effective. Below are some real life examples of how teachers have developed the use of strokes in their work.

Examples of using stroke theory in the classroom

Circle time activities can include giving primary age children practice in giving, accepting and asking for strokes, and in stroking themselves. Here are some ideas to start you off – you will have lots more of your own.

- The use of puppets in circle time can help children look at the way they accept strokes in a way that is non-threatening. A circle time might include a round on what makes children sad in the playground. This information can then be used when introducing a puppet to tell a sad playground story. That is an amalgamation of the worries of the class. The next round then involves the children in problem solving – what they could do to help Sally (the puppet) at playtime, e.g. inviting her to play with them etc. This allows children to talk about the ways that they would like to be helped and stroked through sharing Sally's story.

- Use a puppet or a made up character in a story about all the bad things that could happen to them before school to make them sad. This can also help children talk about things that happen to them. The puppet can have a book put on its head each time someone comes up with a bad/sad thing that could have happened, until the puppet is literally squashed under the weight of all the books. Then the class suggest what they could do to make the puppet character feel better, e.g. share sweets. Each suggestion is followed by a book being lifted off the puppet's head, so releasing him or her to be themselves and happy again. This can also be done on paper by laying on blue sheets of paper each time a bad thing is suggested and then the solutions get the blue paper lifted off to reveal a happy picture of a child. This can be followed up by explaining to children that most people who are bullies are often the ones who have all the bad/sad things happening to them. They need help to change their negative stroking patterns and feel better about themselves. We have done this with Year 7 and 8 pupils as well as primary age, and the activity could be adapted for older pupils.

- Provide opportunities for children to give each other strokes in a safe way, and encourage straight acceptance of strokes without discounting.

  - Say something good about someone else without eye contact or pronouns – one round. 'I think Mel was brilliant at football today.' 'I'm glad Jo is my friend.'
  - Say the stroke to the person without eye contact – second round. 'Mel, you were brilliant in football today.' 'I like being friends with you.'
  - Say it with eye contact – third round. This may take several circle times to complete!

- Make a postbox into which written strokes can be put, then read out in circle time. You may need to check that some children are not missing out by adding some yourself.
- Have a 'boasting mat' which is brought out at least once a week; pupils stand (or jump) on the mat and say something they are pleased about for themselves: 'I am proud I got all my maths questions right', 'I have read 10 pages of my book', 'I swam a width of the swimming bath.' Teachers can reinforce these strokes and encourage children to support each other's achievements. Not all the strokes need to be things that happen at school!
- T-shirts, real ones or paper shapes, can be coloured or painted to advertise what children like about themselves.
- When stroking becomes the norm in a class, children will feel able to ask for strokes they want or need, and to notice if other class members are in need of strokes.
- Have paper 'flower petals' available on which children can write how they feel today and add them to a flower on the wall – an idea for this can be found in the Resources section at the end of Chapter 5.

All these can be done alongside teaching a class about strokes and why they are important.

Case studies

Jill, a behaviour support worker, was consulted by a class teacher about a boy who always reacted badly to praise from the teacher, by disrupting the class, tearing up his work or attacking other children. Jill thought he may have a problem in accepting positive strokes. Working with him and the teacher she devised a way in which he could take charge of his stroke levels; he agreed to put on his table one of a set of symbols (smiley face, sad face, question mark) which would tell his teacher whether he wanted strokes or not.

Brigit has specialised in behaviour support for several years – long enough to be able to trace Year 10 and 11 pupils whom she knew when they were 'disruptive' Year 5s subject to exclusions. With consent from their various schools, and the knowledge that they were all now in stable placements, she asked them to mentor 'problem' pupils through the move from primary to secondary. The group responded with enthusiasm, requested regular 'supervision' from Brigit, and suggested many ideas including talking to parents of their mentees to help them understand the younger pupils' needs.

Josh works pastorally, one-to-one with disruptive pupils. He noticed that one boy, who was showing a great deal of anger, and getting a good deal of attention for it, was not changing at all through anger management techniques. Talking to the boy, he discovered that he had lost three family members through death or departure in the last year. Understanding that anger was the only way this child knew to get strokes, albeit very negative ones. Josh was able to help him accept his sadness. Teachers and midday supervisors, once they recognised the child's situation, responded differently.

Resources

Stroke balance in the classroom (Figure 4.5) (see also Resources section in Chapter 5).

Date ,,,,,,,,,,,,,,,   Class ,,,,,,,,,,,,,,   Lesson ,,,,,,,,,,,,,

During the lesson, or for part of it, put a tick in the appropriate box below when you give someone that type of stroke.

POSITIVE

positive conditional positive strokes for doing something; work – behaviour – attitude.	**positive unconditional** positive strokes of acceptance and respect for pupils – colleagues – support staff, as themselves.
negative conditional negative strokes for doing something; behaviour – attitude – work – etc.	**negative unconditional** negative strokes of rejection or dismissal.

CONDITIONAL (left side) — **UNCONDITIONAL** (right side)

NEGATIVE

What have you learnt about how you give strokes?

Are there differences between the strokes you offer pupils, colleagues, support staff?

Is there anything you want to change?

Figure 4.5 Strokes in class

CHAPTER 5

Emotional Development

- What do children need in order to learn?
- How can schools provide for 'gaps' in development?
- Why do we need a holistic approach to teaching and learning?

In this chapter we will explore a model – cycles of development – which offers a picture of child development that is linked to self-esteem and to the concepts of strokes, discounts and scripts discussed in the previous chapter. The idea that emotional development affects and is part of the learning process is well supported (Goleman 1996; Steiner 1997). This TA-based approach provides practical help for teachers in assessing a child's progress, suggesting helpful teacher/carer interventions for children at different stages, and offering an optimistic and restorative theory to underpin the practicalities of using the concept. Current focus on achievement, and the consequent emphasis on standards and outcomes, sometimes discounts the importance of a more humanistic, student-centred approach that takes the necessity of appropriate support for emotional development as a prerequisite for effective learning (Rogers 1978).

Being your age

Consider the following four 'pen portraits' of children you may meet in nursery or reception class, or if you teach older children focus on the behaviour described rather than the age. For each of them ask:

- What might this child have missed out on that has led to this behaviour?
- What does this child need now in order to help him/her feel secure and enjoy learning?

Louise

Louise is four years old and is in the last term of nursery which she attends each morning. She sometimes finds it difficult to leave her mother when she drops her off at the beginning of the day. This can lead to Louise being difficult to engage in activities for anything up to an hour. She rarely contributes to discussions and when asked questions invariably replies 'Don't know' even though she is an intelligent girl.

There have been no indications of learning difficulty; Louise can present as an interested and able member of the class. However, she appears nervous when tackling new tasks and often refuses to offer answers to questions or suggestions on tackling an activity.

Sasha

Sasha is three years old and has been in the nursery for a couple of weeks. She is extremely difficult to settle into sessions, often cries and wanders around the room. She quickly becomes involved in squabbles with other children and frequently hits or shouts at people around her. Sasha is easily frustrated by tasks and seems to lack concentration, remaining focused for only a couple of minutes before setting off on another tangent.

Liam

Liam is five years old and presents as a very angry little boy. He has few friends and even those relationships are very fragile. He rubbishes his work, spoils the efforts of others and suffers from occasional rages. These outbursts are apparently unprovoked and lead to him swearing at staff and children, pulling material off tables and walls and resisting efforts to calm him. He finds it especially difficult to respond to simple boundaries and resents being told what to do.

Daniel

Daniel is six years old and is considered very immature by staff. He invariably gets into difficulties with other children. This trouble can often arise in the playground when 'play fighting' gets out of hand. Staff are also concerned about his frequent denials when he has clearly upset someone else. Daniel finds it difficult to concentrate in class, often daydreaming or talking with others on off-task themes.

We have used examples of children in the early years; teachers of older children, right up to Year 11, may recognise these behaviours in their pupils too. Again, as you read the following, think in terms of a child's characteristic behaviour, not their actual age.

Ages and stages

These children, like many others, seem not to have had all they need to develop a healthy assurance in relating to other children and finding stimulus and pleasure in their classroom. The work of Piaget, Erickson and others demonstrates that in infancy and childhood development proceeds through a series of identifiable steps or stages. From a TA perspective we know that strokes, unconditional and conditional, are essential to healthy growth and self-esteem, and that based on the strokes they receive, young children make decisions about who they are and how they will interact with others. They also take on board the things they hear 'big people' say about them – clumsy, pretty, slow, cheerful, smart, stupid – and a combination of scores of 'attributions' or labels. By the time they come to school, children have an unconscious picture of themselves and their worth in relation to others. Emotional literacy is defined as the ability to understand your own emotions, to listen to others and empathise with them, and to express emotions productively (Steiner 1997). To begin to achieve a degree of emotional literacy appropriate to their age and development, children may need help to 'restore' the bits they have missed out on – the gaps in their emotional learning that provide the most secure foundation for cognitive learning.

Cycles of development

The cycles of development model was originated by Pamela Levin (1982), who observed and collected data from a number of cultures over several years. The theory that she formulated has two important aspects for each stage of development in the child.

- There are 'tasks' to be completed that are appropriate to each stage and provide the grounding on which the following stage will build. To fully complete these developmental tasks the little person needs certain things from their carers, including 'affirmations', a special kind of stroke effective in enabling the development for that stage. If these are not forthcoming from the main carers and the child cannot get them elsewhere, there will be a deficit in emotional growth which may hinder progress in the next and subsequent stages. The deficit may be small or large and may be due to a range of causes, any of which result in a lack of the right affirmations and so affect the developmental tasks for that stage. The reason may be ordinary – the birth of a sibling, a move, changing relationships in the family – or it may be traumatic. The developmental tasks and the affirmations for each stage are described briefly below, and given in detail later in the chapter.

- In this model, development is not linear but cyclical. This means that we can revisit earlier stages and hopefully find what we need and missed when going through that stage the first time. This applies both to children and to adults; Levin suggests that we do not 'stop' at the end of adolescence but continue to recycle the stages throughout our lives. For children this gives them the chance to 'catch up' on emotional development by hearing, and taking in, affirmations, and practising tasks, for stages earlier than their chronological age. For adults it offers the possibility to 'repair' gaps in development that may have caused difficulties as we recycle in a natural process. Teachers can learn from this model, not just how to help children develop, but what their own needs and 'blind-spots' might be, and so find ways of restoring them (Napper and Newton 2000).

So using this model can be both

- *preventive* – knowing, and providing, what children need in each stage promotes thriving and healthy emotional development

and

- *restorative* – 'repair work' can be done through observation and assessment of possible deficits, and patient and conscientious repetition of needed affirmations.

Levin originally suggested these ideas as a psychotherapeutic approach for working with adults. The educational possibilities were seen and developed by Jean Illsley Clarke (Clarke and Dawson 1998) into a method for parent education based on the preventive and restorative principles above. Clarke expanded the range and number of affirmations, added many ideas about recognising and meeting needs, and offered numerous ways of giving affirmations. The affirmations used in this chapter are based on her work. We believe the ideas can be further developed for teachers and other adults working in schools with children.

Stage 1: Being 0–6 months

From birth to around six months old the baby's primary task is simply to learn to 'be' in the world: to accept care and touch, to bond emotionally, to trust the big people who are taking care of them and to cry out to get needs met. When a baby receives love and care, is handled appropriately and when needs are met consistently, s/he will develop a trusting and responsive attitude which is the basic building block for thriving. This is Erikson's 'basic trust' and is similarly described in the work of Daniel Stern (1998) and object relations therapists. The baby takes in permission 'to be': to trust, to belong and be part of the family, community and humanity. This may sound obvious, but recently we have observed what happens if this basic care is not met: in the 'dying rooms' for girl babies in China, the orphanages of Ceaucescu's Romania and through research on babies and small children in the affluent West. Much less dramatic, but still painful, results can be seen in children such as Louise, who find it hard to trust people, or to belong, and therefore appear passive and uncertain.

This perspective is not about attributing blame to parents – the vast majority of parents offer their children the best care they are able to give. There are many reasons for the lack of needed affirmations – illness in the family, post-natal depression, caring for siblings, accident, trauma, divorce – or simply not knowing what a baby needs through not having had adequate parenting modelled for the parents themselves, for which again there may be understandable reasons. Whatever the reason the result is that a child like Louise, who by her chronological age should be going through the identity Stage 4, seems 'stuck' and unable to move on.

- What does Louise need?
- How can teachers and support workers help her?

Stage 2: Doing (or Exploring) 6–18 months

As the little person becomes mobile, sitting up, crawling, standing, walking, s/he begins to explore the world. The main tasks for this stage are to explore and experience using all the senses, to begin to take initiatives and learn about their world. In order to do so happily children need both protection and encouragement: support in fulfilling their exploratory tasks, which will become a source of experiential learning, the ability to reflect and the development of intuition and sensitive emphatic thinking. The child in this stage is learning an enormous amount, including reading people's expressions and voice tones, making discoveries about his/her own abilities and doing things over and over again until they are 'worked out'. So they need lots of variety, safety from harm and encouragement to explore. While exploring and experimenting, the little person needs to know that a carer is there, and may frequently return to the carer, to reassure themselves, or to share a discovery. Someone who may not have had her needed balance of safety and support is Sasha. Maybe she was too protected and so didn't learn how to explore – or maybe not protected enough so that she had no reference point or safety net in her exploring and got scared.

- What does Sasha need now to build her confidence in exploration and go through this stage now?

Stage 3: Thinking 18 months–3 years

The previous doing stage is about learning to explore without the need to 'structure' experience by using language. As the little person begins to talk, and converse, s/he also comes to see her/himself as a separate person, with his/her own thinking, ideas, feelings and viewpoint. This is the stage of the 'terrible twos' characterised by struggle, conflict and frustration as the child tests reality (and care-givers), wants to do things themselves and has powerful reactions to every new experience. The 'tasks' for this stage are to learn to think and solve problems, and to express feelings. The child needs affirmations for thinking, explanations, 'how to's and clear limits – learning about structure is important at this stage. Two-year-olds are constantly experimenting and testing 'with a passion' both things and people (Gopnik *et al.* 1999), and with the appropriate affirmations in place might even sometimes become the 'terrific' instead of 'terrible' twos. Liam it seems has lacked the structure he needed and so at five years old is still experiencing frustration and chaotic feeling-thinking confusions as a result.

- How can Liam learn to think for himself and let others do the same?

Stage 4: Identity and Power 3–6 years

By three years old the child has made some important decisions about themselves and how they relate to others. During this stage they will further develop these decisions by asking fundamental philosophical questions such as 'Who am I?' 'Who are all those others?' 'What's going on here?' 'What will I do tomorrow?' 'What will I do when I grow up?' The answers they find to these questions become the foundation of the script. The developmental tasks of this stage are to become a separate person with their own identity, to find out who they are, to test their power and find out results of behaviour and to learn to separate fantasy from reality. Stories, books, videos are important in providing information and models in addition to those offered by care-givers and older siblings. Affirmations focus on enabling the little person to be themselves, to be appropriately powerful and to know the difference between real and pretend. By the end of this stage children will be in school – for some, like Daniel, this will happen before they are emotionally ready and when they have not yet arrived at a confident sense of identity.

- What will help Daniel to carry out the tasks for this stage and 'catch up' on his development?

Stage 5: Skills and Structure 6–12 years

This stage encompasses the primary school years during which children learn how to live out their own script story. The social context of school provides a stage on which the script drama can be played out. Social learning is a major component of the tasks for this stage – how to learn from mistakes, how to decide what to do, what the rules are, how to disagree and how to develop a personal value and belief system. Affirmations are needed for all this learning, and reassurance that the children can be different from care-givers and still be valued and appreciated.

Stage 6: Integration 12–18 years

Secondary school age is the time for integrating the learning from all the previous stages by revisiting them and maybe making some adjustments. This will be made more possible by affirmations for growing into adulthood and beginning to exercise independence. This group needs encouragement and support as they go through this revisiting, with sometimes seemingly random behaviour. The 13-year-olds may swing between passivity and activity as they revisit the being and doing stages; 14-year-olds replay the defiance and frustration of the thinking stage as they begin to break away from childhood patterns of behaviour; 15–16-year-olds experience identity problems and 17–18-year-olds again pass through a stage of learning new skills and new rules, this time those of the adult world. At the same time the secondary age pupil will still be playing out any behaviour difficulties associated with gaps in childhood developmental stages, and these may be exacerbated as they revisit stages that they 'missed out' the first time.

Recycling and Change

As we reach adulthood we continue to recycle the stages. Consider, as you look at the affirmations at the end of this chapter, which ones seem important to you. These may be key messages for you personally, either for a stage you are passing through in your natural cycle or for a stage which is significant for you from your own development.

In addition to revisiting the stages as we grow older, we cycle through them whenever we encounter a new or unfamiliar experience such as starting a new job, joining a training course, moving house or starting a new relationship. These are the little spirals on the diagram in Figure 5.1.

Any stages that have significance for us may show up on these little cycles too. One way of exploring this process further is to draw the progression through the stages as a graph of competence and energy, variously known as the change, transition or competence curve shown in Figure 5.2 (Hay 1996).

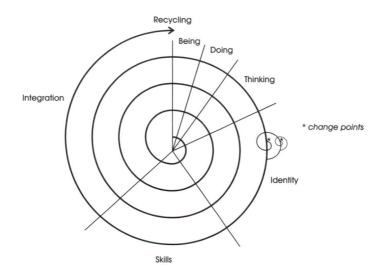

Figure 5.1 The cycle of development (Hay 1993)

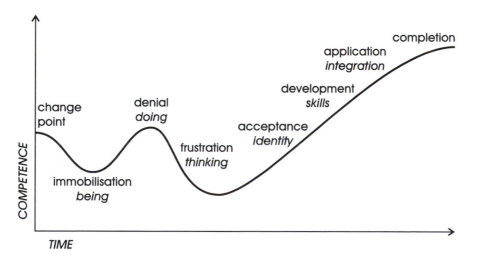

Figure 5.2 The competence curve (Hay 1996)

We can use this graph to describe what happens to a child starting a new school, a teacher starting a new job, or a school going through a process of change. Here, as we go through the stages, think about:

- your own experience of starting something new
- a child you know moving to a new school or being reintegrated
- a child who has recently experienced some change or loss.

As we encounter any new situation there may be an initial sense of confusion, shock or disturbance. This is *immobilisation* on the graph – energy drops and we may become passive as we take in what it means to *be* in this new place; like being 'born into' the unfamiliar situation. Just like a new baby we need to be welcomed and helped to feel we belong.

As we settle in energy rises and we begin to *explore* our new surroundings. Our competence seems to rise too; this may be because we are using skills brought from our previous job or school. We may be *denying* the realities of the new circumstances, that our previous skills or strategies are not enough. To benefit from this phase we need the chance to explore in our own way, without being restricted by imposed expectations, while someone else keeps watch for safety issues. This is a 'feeling' stage, and only when we have a sense of security will we be ready to move on.

Next our energy and sense of competence may drop as we experience the *frustration* characteristic of the *thinking* stage; we now recognise the need to do things differently in our new place but don't yet know how. Encouragement for our own thinking will enable us to take steps towards finding our new *identity*, *accepting* the new environment and our place in it and so moving on to *develop* the *skills* and competence we need now.

Case studies

To illustrate how this model can inform work in schools we can consider the following examples of how the early stages were addressed during reintegration.

Carl was being reintegrated from a special school for pupils with social, emotional and behavioural needs (SEBN) into a local secondary school. It was decided that he should reintegrate at the point of phase transfer so that he would be less conspicuous as a new arrival to the school. Towards the end of his last term at the special school, teachers supported him in having part-time sessions at a local mainstream primary school so that he could become familiar again with the experience of mainstream classes.

After Carl had secured a place at the secondary school he made informal visits with the support from staff based at the special school. He was also involved in the main visits for all pupils transferring to the school. Most importantly the receiving school made it clear that he was welcome and that he was entitled to a place at the school.

During the initial stages of his placement at the new school, staff from the special school continued to support him during his first term so that any anxieties or difficulties could be swiftly addressed. Carl was thus supported through the first three stages (being, doing and thinking) by being welcomed, given the chance to explore his new place, and helped with the transition to accepting his new status.

Another example is Sari, a primary aged pupil who was being reintegrated into a new school following a permanent exclusion. Sari and her parents were invited to a planning meeting that involved several professionals in addition to the school head teacher and class teacher. It was clear that Sari was overwhelmed by the number of adults, which triggered the head teacher to make a powerful move. The head invited Sari to come with her and look around the classrooms where she would be working. Together they went on a tour of the school while the other adults continued their discussions. Later the head teacher and Sari returned and it was suggested that Sari take her mother on a tour of the school.

In both cases some of the key affirmations associated with the *being* stage were delivered through the actions, planning and language of the adults. Using affirmations does not have to involve complex planning – they can simply be reflected in what we say to children.

The cycles of development model helps us to understand the stages of emotional growth in both children and adults. Children who hear, or receive in other ways, the appropriate affirmations are enabled to build positive scripts and so create their own security, encouragement, problem-solving skills, cooperation with others, enjoyment and spontaneity. The affirmations capture the messages we all need (with an emphasis on different ones at different stages) to help us grow and flourish as emotionally literate beings. To accept them ourselves, and to offer them to pupils, takes account of personal, group (class), and organisational (school) needs for thriving and success.

Discounting our needs

Sometimes this doesn't happen. In the last chapter we briefly discussed discounting, the diminishing or belittling of some aspect of a person or situation. Discounting of the emotional needs of pupils can happen in many ways, and like all discounting can take place at four levels. We may discount:

- the existence of a problem – not noticing, or denying, the evidence e.g. ignoring Louise's passivity, or Liam's anger
- the significance of the problem – not accepting the meaning e.g. 'it doesn't mean anything, s/he's just that sort of child'
- the solvability of the problem – not seeing options e.g. 'if that's the way s/he is there's nothing you can do'
- personal power to solve the problem – not taking responsibility e.g. 'I can't think what to do with him/her'.

Taking account of the evidence and its meaning, finding solutions and acting on them is an empowering process for both teacher and pupil.

For Louise, reassurance that she is welcomed and accepted, that her feelings are OK and that others will think for her for a while could provide the security to help her move on. For Liam, consistent limits, strokes for his thinking and acceptance of his feelings will facilitate his progress through the thinking stage.

With both these children – and with all young children – permission to experience themselves as they are, rather than taking on other people's definitions of them, are of paramount importance. Carole Gesme (1996) developed 'pink permissions' (because they are printed on pink card!) to use in giving children permission to accomplish and to feel. Carole discovered, while working in a family treatment centre, that young children found it easier to accept permission to feel (you can feel sad) than to make a statement about their feelings (I feel sad); often they did not know what they were feeling. A list of pink permissions and some ideas for using them can be found at the end of this chapter (under Resources).

Keeping on track: the Structure/Nurture Highway

This tool, shown in Figure 5.3, was developed for parents by Jean Illsley Clarke; we think it is a good model for teachers too. The lanes of the highway are the OK functioning where teachers take account of pupils' needs for support and care, and agree negotiable and non-negotiable rules to provide necessary structure. The 'soft shoulders' are the areas we may stray into under pressure when discounting our ability to do anything to change a stressful situation. If we find ourselves in the dangerous 'marshy grass' at the extremes of the picture we need to take action to alert ourselves and others to our distress and need for help, or we may need someone else to bring it to our attention. This can help us stay alert to the need to:

- stay in the driving lanes
- be aware of when we are on the shoulders and have options for getting ourselves back onto the lanes – take account of our own needs as well as those of the pupils
- keep a balance of structure and nurture in our teaching
- get help from a colleague when we find ourselves near the marshland.

Some ideas for using the highway can be found in the Resources section at the end of this chapter.

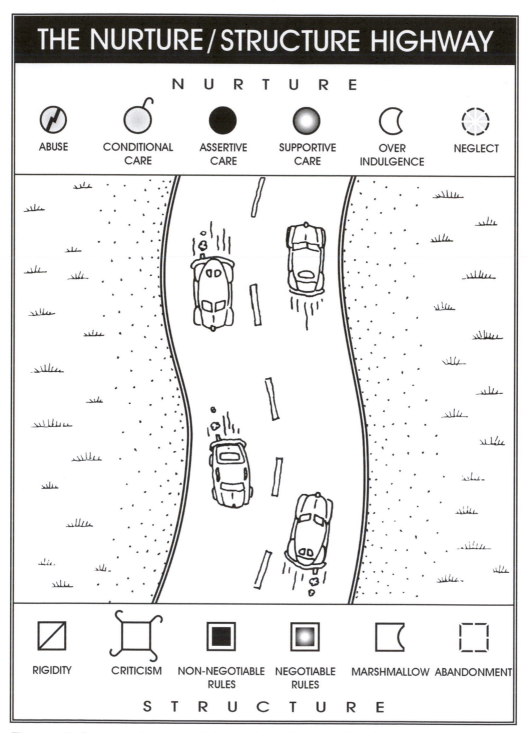

Figure 5.3 Structure/nurture highway, from *Growing Up Again* by Jean Illsley Clarke and Connie Dawson. © 1998, J.I. Clarke and C. Dawson. Reprinted by permission of Hazelden Foundation, Center City, MN.

Case studies

An increasing number of children are communicating through their behaviour that the system is not adequately meeting their needs or enabling them to cope with the pressures of the classroom. One local education authority (LEA) through its primary behaviour support team (PBST) and SEN advisory teacher is developing alternative provision based on the cycles of development model. These are held in three schools one afternoon a week when children of varying ages, all of whom are displaying signs of having missed earlier emotional development, are given access to a nurture session. This consists of a small group with two adults who are available to play with them, read stories, cook, do art activities, role play and just watch over them to keep them safe. The emphasis is on free play and choice. Children are allowed to be and do as they want within the boundaries of safety. The session is drawn to a close with a story. The results of the initial group have been very positive. The sessions are staffed by one member of the PBST and a member of the school staff, who is to continue after the PBST has withdrawn. One member of school staff was so impressed by the way the children had responded to the session that she offered to come into school on her afternoon off if that meant the group could continue. Class teachers are also appreciating that these children are more able to cope in class with this time for them built into the week.

These schools are piloting a session once a week for an afternoon, when children with gaps in their emotional development are being given access and opportunity to do and be affirmed in earlier stages of development. All age ranges are involved including a junior, infant and primary school. The children get time out and access to tasks from earlier stages. Although this is only just developing the early signs are promising. This is to be written into the LEA's Behaviour Support Plan.

Paul is a child who, due to neglect, had missed lots of adult contact in early life. Nursery staff used cycle of development theory to look at what affirmations and tasks he needed to revisit. They used 'growing up again' material, particularly parent behaviours that would be helpful. Paul had spent a lot of time in a room alone watching TV so his mechanical language was quite good. However he did not have the subtleties of communication with others. So the staff members took him back to being and worked on physical touch, mirroring facial expressions, close contact reading etc. and did the same with doing and thinking tasks. The teacher and her head had just been on an early years staff training day on cycles of development so they took it from there.

There are also a number of individual children of primary school age recognised by the PBST as having gaps in their emotional development. Team staff have set up times for these children to work and help in early years and nursery environments. Here they are helping and at the same time playing and so filling in missing gaps and undone tasks. They are also raising their self-esteem through helping others.

We have also worked with many Year 11 pupils who have had gaps in their emotional development who, when on work experience in primary schools and nurseries, have responded very well and been good at playing with the children even when they were considered very disruptive in secondary school.

The use of outdoor education with older pupils with emotional and behavioural difficulties (EBD) is very effective because it gives opportunities for recycling in a context that is not seen as 'babyish'. In fact it is seen as very credible and yet it takes pupils back to tasks associated with those first stages of development. You can play with water in a canoe, you can get muddy and it's OK to be scared and rely on others. Adventure activities are all about perceived risk. The instructor or adult is in control and yet the pupil often feels out of control. They have to trust and so learn to trust. This can be the first time an adult has kept them safe in a way they have not experienced back in their early stages of development.

Resources

The following pages set out the developmental tasks, needed affirmations and helpful teacher/carer behaviours for each stage of development. Table 5.1 gives a convenient summary of these. They are followed by assessment sheets for each stage, which give a means of checking a child's progress in achieving the tasks.

Cycles of development: Stage 1 – Being (0–6 months)

Job of the child:

- To call for care
- To cry or otherwise signal to get needs met
- To accept touch
- To accept nurture
- To bond emotionally – to learn to trust caring adults and self
- To decide to live, to be

Affirmations:

- I'm glad you are here
- You belong here
- What you need is important to us
- We are glad you are you
- You can grow at your own pace

- You can feel all of your feelings
- We want you to be here and want to care for you

Helpful teacher/carer behaviours:

- Affirm child in doing the developmental tasks for this stage
- Provide consistent care as needed
- Think for child when required, while monitoring development through the stage
- Use touch, holding, talking, singing – and intuition to decide how and when
- Be reliable and trustworthy
- Get help when unsure how to respond to child

Cycles of development: Stage 2 – Doing (or Exploring) (6–18 months)

Job of the child:

- To explore and experience the environment
- To develop sensory awareness by using all senses
- To signal needs: to trust others and self
- To continue to form secure attachments with parents and/or care-givers
- To get help in times of distress
- To start to learn that there are options and that not all problems are easily solved
- To develop initiative
- To continue Being stage tasks

Affirmations:

- You can explore and experiment and we will support and protect you
- You can do things as many times as you need to
- You can use all of your senses when you explore
- You can know what you know
- You can be interested in everything
- We like you when you are active and when you are quiet
- We like to watch you grow and learn

Helpful teacher/carer behaviours:

- Affirm child in doing developmental tasks for this stage
- Provide a safe environment and protection from harm
- Provide nurturing touch and encouragement

- Say 'yes' more than 'no'
- Offer a variety of sensory experiences
- Listen to the child, especially if s/he is struggling to express something
- Feedback observations of behaviour and model new language
- Respond when child initiates activity

Cycles of development: Stage 3 – Thinking (18 months–3 years)

Job of the child:

- To establish ability to think for self
- To test reality, to push against boundaries and other people
- To learn to think and solve problems with cause-and-effect thinking
- To start to follow simple safety commands: stop, come here, stay here, go there
- To express anger and other feelings
- To separate from parents without losing their security
- To start to give up beliefs about being the centre of the universe
- To continue earlier tasks

Affirmations:

- I'm glad you are starting to think for yourself
- You can say no and push the limits as much as you need to
- It's OK for you to be angry, and we won't let you hurt yourself or others
- You can learn to think for yourself and others can too
- You can think and feel at the same time
- You can know what you need and ask for help
- You can be yourself and we will still care for you

Helpful teacher/carer behaviours:

- Affirm child in doing developmental tasks for this stage
- Help transition from one activity to another
- Give simple clear directions, including basic safety commands
- Be consistent in setting limits and ensuring they are kept
- Accept all child's feelings without getting into win–lose battles
- Give reasons, and provide information to move child on in own thinking
- Stroke thinking by encouragement and celebration
- Expect child to think about own and others' feelings
- Give time for new thinking to develop, e.g. cause and effect

Cycles of development: Stage 4 – Identity and Power (3–6 years)

Job of the child:

- To assert an identity separate from others
- To acquire information about the world, self, body and gender role
- To discover effect on others and place in groups
- To learn to exert power to affect relationships
- To practise socially appropriate behaviour
- To separate fantasy from reality
- To learn extent of personal power
- To continue learning earlier tasks

Affirmations:

- You can explore who you are and find out about others
- You can try out different ways of being powerful
- All of your feelings are OK here
- You can learn the results of your behaviour
- You can be powerful and ask for help at the same time
- You can learn what is pretend and what is real

Helpful teacher/carer behaviours:

- Affirm child in doing developmental tasks for this stage
- Expect child to express feelings and to connect feeling and thinking
- Teach clearly that it is OK to be who you are, and that both sexes and all cultures are OK
- Answer questions accurately, provide information and correct misinformation
- Be clear about who is responsible for what in classroom and playground
- Encourage fantasy while being clear about what is fantasy and what is reality
- Acknowledge and respond to appropriate behaviour

Cycles of development: Stage 5 – Skills and Structure (6–12 years)

Job of the child:

- To learn skills, learn from mistakes and decide to be 'good enough'
- To learn to listen in order to collect information and think
- To practise thinking and doing

- To reason about wants and needs
- To check out family/school rules and structures
- To learn the relevancy of rules
- To experience the consequences of breaking rules
- To disagree with others and still be wanted
- To test ideas and values
- To develop internal controls
- To learn what is one's own responsibility and that of others
- To develop the capacity to cooperate
- To test abilities against others
- To identify with one's own sex

Affirmations:

- You can think before you say 'yes' or 'no'
- You can learn from your mistakes
- You can trust your intuition to help decide what you want to do
- You can find ways of doing things that work for you
- You can learn the rules that help you live with others
- You can learn when and how to disagree
- You can think for yourself and get help instead of staying in distress
- We still want to be with you when we differ and we can learn together

Helpful teacher/carer behaviours:

- Affirm child in developmental tasks for this stage
- Teach conflict resolution and problem-solving skills
- Give lots of strokes for learning, thinking and finding own way to do things
- Encourage skills development
- Be encouraging, enthusiastic, reliable and consistent
- Respect child's opinions and beliefs and allow discussion
- Be clear that mistakes are part of learning
- Challenge negative behaviour and confront discounting
- Encourage participation in rule-making, and be clear about negotiable and non-negotiable rules

Cycles of development: Stage 6 – Integration (12–18 years)

Job of the adolescent:

- To take steps towards independence
- To achieve a clearer emotional separation from family
- To emerge as a separate independent person with own identity and values
- To be competent and responsible for own needs, feelings and behaviours
- To integrate sexuality into the earlier developmental tasks

Affirmations:

- You can know who you are and learn and practise skills for independence
- You can develop your own interests, relationships and causes
- You can grow in your femaleness or maleness and still need help at times
- You can learn to use old skills in new ways
- We look forward to knowing you as an adult
- We trust you to ask for support when you need it

Helpful teacher/carer behaviours:

- Affirm adolescent for doing developmental tasks
- Continue to offer appropriate support
- Accept adolescent's feelings
- Confront unacceptable behaviour
- Be clear about school's position on drugs etc.
- Encourage growing independence
- Expect thinking, problem solving and self-determination
- Confront destructive or self-defeating behaviour
- Celebrate emerging adulthood, personal identity etc.
- Negotiate rules and responsibilities

(All cycles of development lists are adapted from Clarke and Dawson 1998.)

Stages of development summary chart

	Stages	Tasks of child	Needs, Strokes	Helpful behaviours
1	Being 0–6m	learn to get needs met; learn to trust; bond emotionally; accept care, touch	love, care, touch; consistency; you belong here; think for baby	consistent care; use touch, holding, talking, singing; be reliable; think for child as needed
2	Doing (or Exploring) 6–18m	explore and experience; develop senses, initiative; learn to get help; form secure attachment	safety, encouragement, variety, protection, support; don't interrupt; OK to be active, quiet	provide encouragement, safe environment with varied sensory experiences; listen to child; respond and model language
3	Thinking 1½–3yrs	learn to think, test reality, solve problems, express feelings; begin to separate; give up being centre	encourage thinking; give reasons, how-to's; accept feelings; set limits	give clear directions, information; stroke thinking; accept feelings; be consistent
4	Identity and Power 3–6yrs	assert separate identity; acquire info about self, place in family; test power; social behaviour; separate fantasy/reality	both sexes are OK; give info; answer questions; stroke OK behaviour; get own support	answer questions accurately; connect feeling and thinking; be clear about responsibilities; teach acceptance
5	Skills and Structure 6–12yrs	learn skills; make mistakes; listen; reason; rules and structure in and out of family; values; disagree; test ideas; cooperate	lots of strokes; be reliable, clear; offer tools; set rules; allow consequences; challenge behaviour	teach conflict resolution, problem solving; support skills development; respect child's opinions
6	Integration 12–18yrs	separate; be independent, responsible; have own needs, values; integrate sexuality	understand, encourage, accept, support, discuss, celebrate	offer support; confront destructive behaviour; encourage independence; negotiate rules and responsibilities
7	Recycling			

Table 5.1 Stages of development – summary chart.

Assessment charts

Cycles of development: Stage 1 – Being (0–6 months)

Task   *Level 1–10*

To call for care

To cry or otherwise signal to get needs met

To accept touch

To accept nurture

To bond emotionally – to learn to trust caring adults and self

To decide to live, to be

Target task

Supporting affirmations and permissions

New behaviour looked for

New behaviour seen: when, where, with whom

(Adapted from Daunt and Furmage 1999)

Cycles of development: Stage 2 – Doing (or Exploring) (6–8 months)

Task   *Level 1–10*

To explore and experience the environment

To develop sensory awareness by using all senses

To signal needs: to trust others and self

To continue to form secure attachments with parents and/or care-givers

To get help in times of distress

To start to learn that there are options and that not all problems are easily solved

To develop initiative

To continue Being stage tasks

Target task

Supporting affirmations and permissions

New behaviour looked for

New behaviour seen: when, where, with whom

(Adapted from Daunt and Furmage 1999)

Cycles of development: Stage 3 – Thinking (18 months–3 years)

Task   *Level 1–10*

To establish ability to think for self

To test reality, to push against boundaries and other people

To learn to think and solve problems with cause-and-effect thinking

To start to follow simple safety commands: stop, come here, stay here, go there

To express anger and other feelings

To separate from parents without losing their security

To start to give up beliefs about being the centre of the universe

To continue earlier tasks

Target task

Supporting affirmations and permissions

New behaviour looked for

New behaviour seen: when, where, with whom

(Adapted from Daunt and Furmage 1999)

Cycles of development: Stage 4 – Identity and Power (3–6 years)

Task   *Level 1–10*

To assert an identity separate from others

To acquire information about the world, self, body and gender role

To discover effect on others and place in groups

To learn to exert power to affect relationships

To practise socially appropriate behaviour

To separate fantasy from reality

To learn extent of personal power

To continue learning earlier tasks

Target task

Supporting affirmations and permissions

New behaviour looked for

New behaviour seen: when, where, with whom

(Adapted from Daunt and Furmage 1999)

Cycles of development: Stage 5 – Skills and Structure (6–12 years)

Task   *Level 1–10*

To learn skills, learn from mistakes and decided to be 'good enough'

To learn to listen in order to collect information and think

To practise thinking and doing

To reason about wants and needs

To check out family/school rules and structures

To learn the relevancy of rules

To experience the consequences of breaking rules

To disagree with others and still be wanted

To test ideas and values

To develop internal controls

To learn what is one's own responsibility and that of others

To develop the capacity to cooperate

To test abilities against others

To identify with one's own sex

Target task

Supporting affirmations and permissions

New behaviour looked for

New behaviour seen: when, where, with whom

(Adapted from Daunt and Furmage 1999)

Pink permissions for change

- You can help others
- You can tell the truth
- You can be angry
- You know what you are feeling
- You can have fun
- You can ask someone to help
- You can express all your feelings
- You are a terrific person
- You can be a good friend
- You are important
- You can learn the rules

Here are two ideas for using the pink permissions.
- Choose an affirmation that you think will support the child's development using the 'stages' and the assessment charts. Then pick three permissions which relate to it, e.g. for Liam one affirmation might be 'you can know what you need and ask for help'

> permissions 'you are important'
>   'you know what you are feeling'
>   'you can learn the rules'

A teacher or other adult will sit with Liam and read these three times a day, and talk about them, for as long as it takes for Liam to become calmer.
- Make a 'feeling faces board' (or get one from the book *Affirmation Ovals* obtainable from Kevin Smallwood (address at the end of Further Reading)) with balloon faces with many different expressions – sad, happy, worried, angry, scared, laughing, puzzled etc. When a child identifies the face which shows their feelings offer pink 'balloons' (pink permission ovals) for them to choose one to wear, keep in their pocket etc. Talk with the child about their feelings, and give assurance that all feelings are OK. For younger children you will read the permissions to them; older children may want to read them and then choose.

Structure/nurture highway

Teachers, other adults working with children, and parents/care-givers can all use the highway to share difficulties and develop ways of dealing with them. Toy cars can be moved along the road while someone talks about their experience of a child or class and what they want to change in the way they respond; this often results in new insights gained. As an example: Kelly placed her little car on the 'non-negotiable rules' lane, thinking of her Year 6 class and various conflicts about uniform. She realised she often moved onto the 'criticism' shoulder and was in danger of ploughing into 'rigidity'. She took a clue from the 'assertive care' end of this lane and decided to move over to *supporting* the class in *negotiating* rules which would be acceptable to them, Kelly herself, and the school, and could be part of a class contract.

Ways of using affirmations

Each of the developmental stages has an associated colour
being – red   doing – orange   thinking – yellow
identity – green   skills – pale blue   integration – dark blue
and they are often written or printed on an oval shape like Figure 5.4.

Figure 5.4

The ovals can be any size – small ones for giving, larger ones to put on the wall. (Various sizes and sets of affirmation ovals, on stickers or shiny card, can be obtained from Kevin Smallwood, see Further Reading). Many ideas for using the ovals can be found in *Growing up Again* and *Affirmation Ovals* (see Further Reading). Here are just a few:

- Make a poster of affirmations for an age group and put it on the wall; answer questions about them as they are asked.

- Use them in combination with the pink permissions as above (the pink permissions can also be put on pink card ovals, or purchased).
- For smaller children – have affirmations for stages up to the children's own age in a box or on a table; ask children to hand you one of a particular colour, then read it to them.
- Draw 'eggcups' the right size to hold the ovals like an egg (see Figure 5.5) add names, and choose affirmations for each; or let the children choose their own, or for a friend.

Figure 5.5

- Use the ovals as flower petals as in Figure 5.6.

Feelings Flowers

Figure 5.6

CHAPTER 6

Developing a Positive School Culture

- How do others describe your school ethos?
- How do you measure school culture?
- What is the most effective way for changing school culture?

For years commentators, researchers, policy-makers, inspectors, LEA officers and teachers have recognised the significance of having a positive whole-school policy and approach to establishing positive behaviour. Some have endeavoured to determine what this enigmatic phrase might mean – they have attempted to identify the critical factors that make for an effective, positive school ethos that underpins positive relationships within a school community. A handful of studies present a series of factors that expose these apparent secret ingredients, for example, Watkins and Wagner (2000), Galvin *et al.* (1999) and DfEE-funded research focusing on effective provision for pupils with EBD (University of Birmingham 1998). However, for the most part the notion of school culture remains an elusive concept, conjured with smoke and mirrors and references to 'sound leadership', 'consistency', 'raising self-esteem' and the inevitable but bland need for 'high expectations'.

Perhaps one of the most radical applications of TA in education is using its key concepts to assess and develop school culture in a way that is rooted in actual experience of the school. The focus of this section is to explore how the egostate concept can be used in articulating the cultural profile of the organisation with a view to using this as a starting point for developing policy and practice. Much of this discussion will centre on the use of the School Ego-gram Assessment Tool (SEAT) and experience of using this approach with schools. This chapter also considers how other TA concepts covered in previous chapters can be used in reflecting on school development issues. In some respects this is the most challenging part of our work in that it brings into sharp focus the observation that the feelings, experience and behaviour of adults are inextricably linked to the feelings, experience and behaviour of children in the classroom. It may be a provocative claim but it is often the case that making effective progress with difficult behaviour means starting in the *staffroom*, not the classroom. We hasten to add that this is not about apportioning blame, but identifying where our best hopes lie. We believe that schools can change to become even better places where children can achieve in terms of both academic and emotional growth.

Have you ever overheard colleagues from outside your school refer to it as 'friendly' or 'welcoming'? Or perhaps heard a quite different comment – that it's 'an intimidating place', 'business-like' or 'high achieving'? In listening to discussions about schools we hear phrases that are often used in reference to personality: 'Ever since school X went grant-maintained they think they are better than the rest of us', 'The school down the road is exceptionally unfriendly – if you don't fit in you have had it', ' I always enjoy going to school Y, it's a happy place to be', 'They try hard there, at school Z, but they are so disorganised!'

We may only occasionally get glimpses of how others see us, but more importantly we will have a keen sense of what being part of the school means for us on a day-to-day basis. We may be aware that some messages are very powerful in our school – staff may be encouraged to 'be busy' or 'be in control'. It might be that the messages are about being 'neat and tidy' in how we administer our work, or that staff are encouraged to 'take risks, meet new challenges' and 'learn from mistakes'. All organisations, including schools, have key messages – an emphasis that has a distinct resonance for the children and adults working there. The roots of these are most obviously linked to the attitudes and perspectives of senior managers, but there are other significant factors including governors, staff culture and organisational history. In many respects, the school is not dissimilar from any individual teacher or pupil – it has a history, some key influences and a sense of its own identity in the here and now. Like individual people, the school learns to live with itself and in doing so communicates to others what it is about. It is worth remembering that as with people, schools have the capacity to change, either in terms of progression or deterioration.

The 'school egostate' metaphor

We can develop a way of making sense of school culture through using the concept of egostate. In an earlier chapter we considered how individuals have three egostates: Parent, Adult and Child. Each of these can be used to describe what makes up a personality, with unique experiences leading to a distinctive individual profile. As a consequence of this unique history, individuals respond differently to situations, drawing from a number of potential options – some of which are positive, others negative. The perception of others is informed by their experience of the behavioural modes and generates judgements about whether the individual is friendly, business-like, good fun, eccentric or just annoying.

Organisations too have unique histories that shape what has been possible in the past, which in turn informs what is permissible in the present. We can use the metaphor of egostates to describe their behaviours and how these in turn communicate meaning to others. When we refer to school ethos or culture, we can understand this in terms of the 'messages' that the organisation gives out both to those within it and to those outside it.

As part of our own development – both as a child and in our ongoing grown-up processing – we learn how we can be OK with ourselves and others, or not as the case might be. This experience can lead to a predominant egostate that feeds into how we behave generally. We may tend to feel most comfortable when we are in control and when there are clear boundaries structuring our work or relationships. On the other hand we may generally respond more effectively when there is a high level of flexibility and an emphasis on spontaneity. Often we have certain egostates that inform how we think, pre-empt and respond in relating to others. For most of us, for most of the time we have become familiar with managing who we are.

We can consider the school, at an organisational level, as also having preferred egostates. This means that for a number of reasons, school behaviour is informed by its distinct personality profile. A school's behaviour is particular to itself – there may be a dozen common local and national features that impact on a number of, or all, schools, but a school's unique history shapes its behaviour.

One approach is to use a school egostate plan. The plan has been designed around the five main egostate modes and colleagues are invited to cite examples of activity that can be associated with each. The objective is to build up a sense of what the school does that reflects its capacity to draw from specific egostates. An example of a school with a well-developed, autonomous profile is provided in Figure 6.1.

School Ego-gram Assessment Tool (SEAT)

A more detailed approach, and one that provides useful information for planning potential change is the SEAT.

When working with teachers using the concept of egostates, a number of issues became apparent to us. There is a tendency for staff to overemphasise the need to establish Adult–Adult transactions. Obviously this can be a very useful in working with pupils, especially where there is potential conflict. However, an important, subtle observation is that we might want to draw on a wider range of potential transactions because there are limitations in always aiming for simple Adult–Adult dialogue. For instance, we know that well-timed humour, appropriate nurturing and acknowledging teachers' emotions can all prove effective in responding to situations. Having a more balanced egostate profile is an advantage and has many benefits in providing options for responding, both for individuals and, using our metaphor, for schools. If a teacher's behaviour is dominated by Controlling Parent/Adapted Child, then this limits their capacity in responding to difficulty. Similarly, if a school has a tendency to respond from Controlling Parent, this too will reduce its effectiveness in dealing with problem situations.

Understanding organisations using egostates

Organisation: *CLAYTON PRIMARY SCHOOL*

Detail the features of the organisation in relation to the respective egostates. Try to identify precise and tangible features.

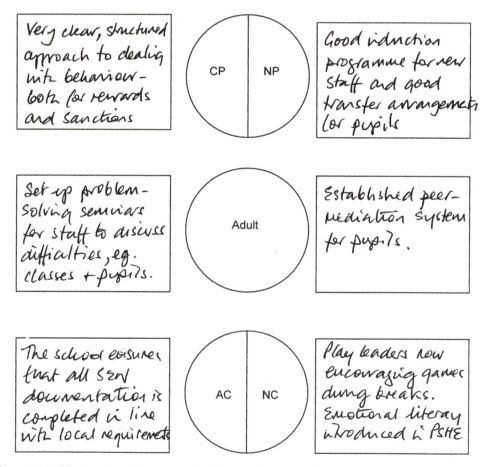

Very clear, structured approach to dealing with behaviour – both for rewards and sanctions

CP | NP

Good induction programme for new staff and good transfer arrangements for pupils

Set up problem-solving seminars for staff to discuss difficulties, eg. classes + pupils.

Adult

Established peer-mediation system for pupils.

The school ensures that all SEN documentation is completed in line with local requirements

AC | NC

Play leaders now encouraging games during breaks. Emotional literacy introduced in PSHE

Figure 6.1 Understanding organisations using egostates

When teachers have started to work with the Parent–Adult–Child (P–A–C) concept questions begin to be raised about what it means in terms of understanding school culture. In response to this question the SEAT has been developed. It is essentially an assessment questionnaire that generates a profile of the school's 'personality'. Similar to personality profiling surveys used for individuals, the SEAT can provide an insight into the school ethos using the egostate model as a reference.

The SEAT proforma is based on a format originally designed by Julie Hay (1996) for use by individuals to get a sense of their own egostate profile. There are a total of 30 items, each one of which is linked to the behavioural modes. The items relate to a wide range of possible attitudes, both helpful and unhelpful, that might describe how the school is perceived. Responses to each item can be weighted so that a varying degree of emphasis can be presented in a summative profile. By adding together the scores for each response it is possible to get a sense of a school's ego-gram. Having achieved this stage of initial assessment the profile can be used to inform further development of school culture.

Using the SEAT

The wider the participation in compiling the school profile, the more valuable the exercise. In some instances an individual member of staff might complete the survey but this is likely to be difficult given the range of items. To involve a full staff team may be time-consuming but it will lead to a more eclectic profile, as opposed to drawing on the perspective of pastoral and senior managers, which is another possible approach. Perhaps some of the most interesting contributions will come from regular visitors to the school – for instance the link educational psychologist, specialist support teacher or education welfare officer.

The proforma takes approximately five minutes to complete and, on the basis of a total response of around 30 forms, an hour to summarise in a final profile. The exercise can form part of a whole-school audit in relation to behaviour, or be used as a discrete activity to inform particular school development work. The survey needs to be put in a local context so that colleagues have an understanding of the purpose of the exercise – referring to the contracting principles in Chapter 3 will be helpful in considering using the SEAT. For example, it would be important to explain to colleagues why the SEAT is being used and how results would feed into further planning.

Clearly one person will be responsible for collating and summarising proformas, however, the task of making sense of the responses and exploring the egostate profile should be shared across as wide a group as possible. Involving others in considering the summative profile is an important part of the process in developing a local understanding of school ethos.

Developing a school ethos

Perhaps the most important aspect of the SEAT approach is that under each item respondents are encouraged to cite evidence to support their response. For example, if a 3 has been given for an item – 'The school responds calmly in a crisis' – the expectation will be that there are good examples to show what this judgement is based on. This could include references to having members of the senior management team patrolling corridors to pre-empt trouble at lunch break, or having a system in place for managing stress prior to an inspection. However, if a 0 or 1 had been given, no evidence is anticipated. The importance of this evidence-based approach is that in addition to generating an egostate profile, the SEAT also provides a comprehensive list describing what activity underwrites current school culture. The implications of this in developmental terms are significant, as illustrated in the example below:

Case study

Ramsey Comprehensive School

Senior staff at Ramsey Comprehensive School wanted to have a closer understanding of their school culture using the SEAT approach. Work was already in hand focusing on the promotion of positive behaviour and relationships between staff and pupils. The intention was to identify what was driving current school culture and consider aspects that might be developed. All staff – teaching and non-teaching personnel – were involved in completing the questionnaires, which were collated by a member of the senior management team.

A total of 33 responses was collated and 80% of all staff canvassed. Almost all responses were made anonymously so it was not possible to differentiate comments across different groups of staff.

The Ramsey School profile is presented in Figure 6.2.

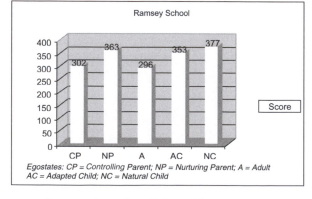

Figure 6.2 Ramsey Comprehensive School Ego-gram

General observations:

- It is important to recognise at the outset that there is no predominant mode. In other words, on the basis of staff perception, the profile presents as well integrated and balanced. In personality terms, we would regard someone with a similar profile as 'grounded' or stable, with a highly developed sense of responding appropriately across a range of circumstances. It suggests that there is a careful balance maintained between the management of, and innovation in, the school climate.
- Interestingly the CP response is relatively low, which is arguably unusual for schools. The legitimate emphasis on control and structure can sometimes extend to intrusive and over-controlling tendencies, particularly in the secondary phase.
- An important feature is the higher response for NC behaviour. Associated with feelings such as anger, sadness and a sense of fun, the NC egostate in this profile is mirrored in the correspondingly high response in NP, which is associated with caring behaviour.
- The lower Adult response suggests that the healthy school ethos may possibly be maintained more by well-founded intuition than on explicit, systematic management mechanisms.

The evidence collated during SEAT exercises makes for both important reading and valuable material for other schools. For instance, if a school profile indicates a low level of Adult responses and this is identified as an area for improvement, a school would do well to consider what other schools have cited as Adult activity that might be used to boost this aspect of school culture. On the other hand, a school may want to safeguard and/or extend, for example, its Natural Child by copying enhancing activities used by other schools. Having used the SEAT approach in the context of a number of schools we have begun to build a list of possible activities that colleagues have cited for items relating to different egostates and these are presented in Table 6.1.

Driving forces

The SEAT profile for a school provides a starting point for developing or changing an organisational culture. The profile presents a snapshot of what the school currently does that both underpins and demonstrates its culture. In addition to using the SEAT approach, another valuable concept from TA can be used to further our understanding of organisational culture – *drivers*.

As individuals develop their scripts, as discussed in Chapters 4 and 5, an important dimension of the process is the emergence of dominant *driver* styles.

Egostate	School Behaviour: Activities, Responses and Evidence

Controlling Parent	• Clearly defined behaviour policy:
	  • Specific procedures
	  • Onus on pupils taking responsibility for their own actions
	  • Use of daily behaviour plans
	• School informs parents through weekly and termly reports in addition to regular meetings and phone calls
	• School staff are encouraged to deliver INSET at other schools
	• School staff invited to take positions on LEA committees
	• Staff tend to refer back to previous experience when solving problems
	• Parents/carers advise to keep school informed about changing pupil circumstances
	• Staff encouraged to visit other centres/schools to advise on practice
	• SMT on-call system for picking up on pupils sent out of class
	• Clear guidance for pupils and staff for movement around the school
	• Detentions held every break-time, managed via staff rota
	• Initial home–school arrangements are established on first visit to school to make clear expectations
	• The school tends to do its own thing operating autonomously from the LEA
	• Sanctions and rewards reinforced through displays in playground and classrooms
	• IEPs give clear messages about expectations
	• The school refers back to the experience of others in dealing with difficulty
	• The school has been regarded as a centre for excellence in terms of subject status
	• Behaviour policy in place as a result of OFSTED action plan
	• Emphasis on uniform regulations

Nurturing Parent	• Staff generally available and approachable • Clear targets in terms of Individual Education/Behaviour Planning • Staff work to improve pupils' self-esteem • School establishes a non-judgemental, 'fresh start' approach to issues • The unit intake is predominantly comprised of excluded pupils • Staff encouraged to advise, not criticise pupils • Pupils encouraged to 'open up' in relation to talking about difficulty • The school endeavours to create a safe environment for pupils • Staff work closely with parents and pupils at induction to explain school objectives • Support staff are encouraged to play a mediation role • The school makes good arrangements for pupils with EAL and refugees • As a result of having places the school tends to take in excluded pupils and refugees • Excellent preparation of pupils prior to transition from primary phase • First aid room readily available • Peer mentor system using older pupils to support younger pupils • Bullying council made up of each age group based on 'no-blame' style approach • Flexible working arrangement with behaviour support service in problem solving for pupils with EBD • Nurturing ethos; high value placed on building positive relationships between school, home and children • Buddy system in place for new pupils

	• Assessment policy emphasises the developmental • Staff and pupil potential are developed through the curriculum and staff training programme • Breakfast clubs for pupils • School brochure provided at induction • Weekly meetings to support induction of new pupils
Adult	• Members of staff are generally available to pick up issues that spill out of classrooms • Staff use IEPs/IBPs as part of a problem-solving approach • Maintaining calm approach as a crucial element in working with pupils with EBD • School seeks information on new initiatives to assess impact and implications for school • The school recognises that a problem-solving approach is best maintained within a relaxed atmosphere • The school has distinct but flexible boundaries regarding behaviour and learning • All sides of the situation are explored prior to bringing all parties together to resolve difficulty • Flexible systems for meeting individual needs through problem solving • At times of crisis the school takes a step-by-step approach, preferring a preventive option • A stable working environment is underpinned by a clearly defined daily routine • Developments for the school are regularly taken to staff for consultation • The role of SMT in calmly managing crisis is seen to be crucial • Regular meeting between head teacher and pupils negotiating daily targets • School holds multi-agency meetings with parents • Introduction of mentoring in collaboration with social services • Problem solving is addressed through INSET and staff meetings • Time and resources committed to SEN, multi-agency liaison • Adopt an ecosystemic approach to problem solving • Few exclusions indicate calmness in managing crisis • School seeks out information regarding new initiatives, i.e. use of PSPs, SEN and EBD • External agencies are used in a facilitative role
Adapted Child	• Curriculum guidance and timetabling is within prescribed DfEE expectations • Length of school day reflects DfEE guidance • School use interview approach in liaising with parents and visitors • School adopts a respectful and fair approach to meeting with parents and visitors • School adapts external demands to the needs of pupils • School follows external guidance regarding SEN assessment and recording • School works on the basis of treating visitors as expected to be treated in return • The school uses LEA guidance manuals for developing aspects of work • Fully incorporating the literacy framework • School has due regard for inspection framework and advice from LEA advisory staff • LEA advisors tend to lead on developing new initiatives and setting expectations • Introduction of 'booster classes' and the prioritisation of achievement over special needs, teaching to SATs all in response to local and national agendas • Consistent welcome and courtesy across all staff • School takes LEA guidance as a basis for developing school-based practice

	• School takes a contrary position on exclusion appeals • The school ethos is centred around maintaining the status quo • School uses pupil 'welcomers' • Generating action plan as a result of OFSTED inspection • Range of polite notices displayed around the school
Natural Child	• Links made with following agencies: EWS, EPS, social services, YOTs, parents, local community groups, health services, careers service, colleges, traveller education service, parent helpers, youth service • High level of pupil attendance indicating a sense of enjoyment with school • A happy staffroom • Enjoyment is regarded as an important part of behaviour development • Established a volunteer reading support scheme • Representation on how school feels in relation to issues made to LEA • Inter-tutor group competitions • Staff/pupil barbecues • The school was the first to introduce Academic Tutoring and student interviews • School challenges 'experts' in meetings and defends school interests • The school tends to be creative on issues which are problematic • Wide range of extra curricular clubs for pupils at lunchtime and after school • Staff celebrations organised by staff committee • Established culture of openness in the staffroom • Use of local media to articulate school perspective • Restructuring playtimes and decorated school • Staff meals out and social evenings

Table 6.1 Evidence from SEAT questionnaire

These are the messages that individuals pick up as children that offer a 'conditional OK-ness'. In other words, we learn that we will be OK if we adopt one, or a combination, of the driver messages:

- *I'll be OK if I stay strong*
- *I'll be OK if I hurry up*
- *I'll be OK if I please others*
- *I'll be OK if I can be perfect*
- *I'll be OK if I try hard*

These driving forces emerge particularly when we find ourselves in stressful situations and our behaviour, language and gesture can often indicate to others which driver we are using. Drivers affect the way we work, both alone and with others; Julie Hay (1993) refers to them as *working styles*. As our characteristic styles of working each has both benefits and drawbacks for us. With experience we can learn to manage the 'downside' of our typical behaviour and enjoy the benefits it brings, individually and as team members.

- Be Perfect: People with this working style achieve a high standard of detailed work because they want everything to be right. For them the most important thing is to do the job well, with no errors, and they tend to feel low or 'unworthy' if they don't reach their own standard of excellence. Often they will fail to meet deadlines because they need to do everything perfectly. They are great at checking nothing has been missed, and will plan ahead and be well organised. Others may find them intimidating or 'de-skilling'. When they can accept that sometimes 'good enough' is good enough they can relax a little and still enjoy their ability to produce fine work.

- Be Strong: These people are seen as calm and reliable, great in a crisis and known 'copers'. They will carry on when everyone else is despairing and so things may get dumped on them because they are unlikely to object. Sometimes others may wonder if they really are doing all the jobs they have taken on. They find it difficult to share their problems and anxieties so may work to the stage where they collapse. If they can ask for help when they need it, rather than when it is almost too late, and accept available support, relationships with colleagues will improve and the benefits of their even-tempered style be appreciated.

- Please People: The overriding need for these people is to please others so they will often 'mind read' and do things for other people without first checking that it is wanted or needed. They are concerned to create harmony and find it hard to deal with dissent so they are great team members, taking care of others' needs and maintaining a social as well as work perspective. They are often smiling and cheerful, and may 'wonder' rather than ask directly, and will rarely assertively refuse jobs because others' priorities are more important than their own. They are pleasant, empathic and caring, generally nice to have around because they notice what is going on and what other people need. When they can also pay attention to their own needs they can enjoy their people skills without over-burdening themselves.

- Try Hard: These people are full of energy and enthusiasm for new projects, great motivators and creatively active. They will initiate and take a can-do attitude, often volunteering before anyone else to try an interesting new approach. However their enthusiasm may go into trying rather than succeeding, and their ability to see all possibilities means that they often fail to complete a task and others have to move in to pick things up. Their weakness is in lack of planning and getting carried away by their ardour; when they can learn to plan and enjoy completing projects they can be invaluable for their positive energy.

- Hurry Up: For these people the main aim is to do things now, or at least very soon. They pressurise themselves and others by doing too many things at once and all in a hurry. In fact, when they can allow themselves time, they can be very efficient, getting through an enormous amount of work because their energy peaks under pressure. If they don't take time they risk making mistakes, and so losing time because something has to be done again. They tend to not start projects until the deadline is near because they actually enjoy the 'busy-ness' and their ability to think fast. This can be irritating for colleagues, who know that the approach of a deadline means pressure for them too. When Hurry Ups can let themselves take time and prioritise appropriately, their efficiency and quick thinking can benefit everyone.

Of course human beings are not so straightforward as to fit neatly into one category – most of us have a combination of these styles – but we all generally have one where we tend to go under pressure. The two tables show the strengths and limitations of the five styles (Table 6.2) and examples of how permissions can be helpful for teachers (Table 6.3)

Driver	Strengths	Limitations
Be strong	Can put others' needs before one's own to manage difficult situations	Not acknowledging own needs leads to overload/withdrawal
Hurry up	Can meet tight deadlines, covering a significant amount of work	Generates unnecessary pressure on self and others, can result in errors
Please others	Can be invaluable in developing teamwork; intuitive of others' needs	Can deny own needs and wants linked to a sense of poor self-worth
Be perfect	Can lead to a very high standard of work and high expectation of others	Can be intolerant of own work and that of others that is 'good enough'
Try hard	Can be valuable in enthusing and energising self and team	Can become preoccupied with 'trying' and not complete task

Table 6.2 Driver strengths and limitations

We may recognise ourselves in one or more of the above driver positions. We can also observe driver behaviour in other people. This may be indicated through what people say, but also through how they behave. It is important to remember that driver behaviour becomes most prevalent during times of stress and is essentially ways in which individuals maintain a sense of how they will be able to survive the situation. This concept is presented in the illustration below (Figure 6.3). The driver 'balloons' rescue us from drowning as the self-limiting parts of the script pull us down into the water.

In the same way that drivers and associated working styles can be used to understand aspects of individual personality, so we can use the concept to illuminate organisational ethos. All schools will have driver messages and resulting working styles which manifest the cultural script of the organisation. Imagine a school where the working style is:

Driver	Helpful permissions	Example
Be strong	It is OK to be strong and to also acknowledge individual needs	An experienced teacher allowing themselves to say that they have had a difficult time with a class
Hurry up	It is OK to give time to reflect on what is being done	A member of staff with the task of drafting an anti-bullying document deciding to take time in carrying out an audit of need
Please others	It is OK sometimes to meet individual needs and wants	A teacher signs out a video they need rather than ask everybody in the department if they want to use it
Be perfect	It is OK sometimes to complete a task that is good enough	A class teacher giving pupils an opportunity to peer assess work rather than meticulously mark the work herself
Try hard	It is OK to complete a task at an initial attempt	A class teacher deciding that a display of children's work designed by the class is good enough

Table 6.3 Driver permissions

- Be Perfect: the school which judges itself by the standards it sets and reaches, with an emphasis on academic achievement and an expectation that things will be done 'the right way'. This may show up in a level of excellence, and also in firm uniform regulations and general neatness.
- Be Strong: a solid, reliable place without a great deal of creativity or excitement, where things go on more or less satisfactorily and the work gets done. However there is little acknowledgement of feelings, either of staff or pupils, and everyone is simply expected to 'get on with it' whatever the demands.
- Please People: comes over as a 'warm' school, with lots of colour, displays of pupils' work, plenty of activities, maybe a strong community base and high level of parental involvement. May be seen as lacking in rigour or challenge to pupils' achievement.
- Try Hard: the school which radiates enthusiasm but sometimes fails to live up to it, maybe by running too many activities so that the energy runs out when it comes to seeing things through. When working well, good at motivating staff and pupils and getting new projects up and running.
- Hurry Up: there may be a general sense of hurry and pressure and few or no opportunities to reflect on how and why policies or activities are implemented. At its best this school will be efficient and achieve a lot, but less robust pupils and staff may feel (and be) neglected.

Figure 6.3 (From an idea by Adrienne Lee)

Consider the scenario where a school has just been notified of the date of its next inspection. Understandably there will be a degree of anxiety about what the process might involve, concerns about the outcome of the inspection and worries about the lead up to the actual visit. How might different driver behaviours look? Table 6.4 provides some ideas.

School inspection is an obvious example of where an organisation may feel under pressure, but there will be other occasions where stress emerges:

- specific difficult situations involving parents
- pupil exclusion, local developments, e.g. school reorganisation, LEA inspection, education budget-setting exercise
- national issues, e.g. performance management, social inclusion agenda, raising pupil achievement, teacher recruitment, initiative overload.

Becoming aware of driver behaviour is an important step towards utilising the benefits of the associated working style and so minimising limitations. At an individual level it can be valuable to recognise and consciously use our style of behaviour to manage difficult situations. For example, a teacher with a dominant 'Be strong' style may use this to cope with a cover lesson of an unfamiliar and

Driver	Helpful messages/behaviour	Unhelpful messages/behaviour
Be strong	Senior management decision to take on bulk of organisational tasks enabling teaching staff to work with minimal distraction	Minimal acknowledgement of how staff might be feeling about the inspection
Hurry up	Staff work efficiently to get the necessary tasks done, sense of challenge in meeting deadlines	Pressure to get things done to unrealistic targets, mistakes take extra time and work to put right
Please others	Emphasis on presenting the school at its best in terms of displays, decoration and documentation	Overemphasis on accommodating the inspection process at the expense of ongoing school development issues – allowing the inspection to sidetrack school's purpose
Be perfect	Emphasis on high expectations of pupils and staff in terms of work and behaviour. Time spent on reviewing and improving documentation and policies	Unrealistic expectations about perfection where difficulties exist and/or unexpected situations can occur. Unhelpful pressure on colleagues and pupils
Try hard	Pre-inspection period generates an enthusiasm and motivation for the challenge, and planning to cover all aspects ready for inspection	Colleagues invest significant time and energy into a range of activities that is either poorly coordinated or where little opportunity is given to reflect on progress

Table 6.4 Drivers under inspection

difficult class. Another teacher might use their 'Be perfect' style in preparing a new set of materials for a class. At an individual level it can be equally useful to identify when driver behaviour is becoming unhelpful, for example where a teacher's 'Hurry up' results in having no opportunity to consider their teaching effectiveness.

Similarly, we can consider the extent to which school behaviour is driven by specific driver behaviour and reflect on the extent to which it might be best used in times of difficulty.

- What issues are pressurising your school at the moment?
- What *unhelpful* driver behaviour have you observed?
- How could the *positive* aspects of the school's working style help?

In considering changing an emphasis in behaviour we need to focus on using permissions that challenge some of the injunctions that inform driver behaviour. Consequently, in reflecting on responses to the second question above, the following may be useful:

- What permissions might be helpful for you?
- What permissions might you find useful in working supportively with colleagues?
- What kind of permissions might be most helpful in developing school culture?

Moving to autonomy

Eric Berne (1964: 158–60) defined autonomy as having:

- Awareness of ourselves, others and situations.
- The ability to react spontaneously from a range of options.
- The capacity for intimacy (closeness or openness).

At a personal level autonomy can be connected with an 'I'm OK, You're OK' perspective. Similarly, schools can also choose to move to autonomy by using all their organisational egostates. Below are some examples of what an autonomous school might include:

- Taking care of staff and pupils, perhaps through the Healthy Schools Initiative.
- Providing a well-defined structure for maintaining good behaviour, for example the use of circle time.
- Sound understanding of the school's strengths and weaknesses, perhaps identified through systematic self-review.

- A commitment to responding to challenge, for example in setting up an effective on-site centre for supporting staff *and* pupils.
- Arrangements for acknowledging the impact of experiential learning and the importance of emotional literacy.

In many respects this book has been all about encouraging teachers, non-teaching staff and schools to become autonomous. Our aim has been to focus on increasing colleagues' awareness of the impact of thinking and behaviour on that of others. The resources have been designed to heighten sensibilities regarding relationships and encouraging ways of working most effectively within a given context. The consideration of emotional growth and development is a theme that runs through all the chapters and this has been intentional, promoting the possibility for intimacy within the context of a classroom or school.

Each of us has choices at a personal level as well as professionally. Often we will not be conscious of the choices we are making – they are informed by well-established and deeply ingrained perceptions of how the world works. Consequently much decision making can appear as 'intuitive' or 'common sense' practice. However, invariably there are options and, for most of the time, at a personal level, this generates some type of benefit for us. A metaphorical illustration is where our person in Figure 6.3 struggling to remain above the waterline, buoyed up by the driver balloons, is now able to swim freely and make choices as to which island they might want to visit (see Figure 6.4).

Figure 6.4 (From an idea by Adrienne Lee)

When we consider autonomy at a whole-school level, there is an additional degree of complexity. The school has its own, organisational world-view that is underwritten by its particular history and experience. Within the school community there will be individuals who have their own particular version of that organisational experience in addition to their individual perspective on the world. Becoming an autonomous school has some inherent complexities and tensions that should not be underestimated!

The most important message is that because of the richness of school communities and therefore the potential for difficulty, it is even more important that processes for making decisions are a prominent and explicit feature in all planning and communication. At the heart of Berne's definition of autonomy lies the integrated Adult, the most powerful and effective base from which to work, live and grow with others. Learning new behaviour patterns is part of this integration process. 'Transactionally, this means that anyone functioning as an Adult should exhibit three kinds of tendencies: personal attractiveness and responsiveness, objective data processing, and ethical responsibility' (Berne 1961: 195). Drawing on what is useful from our previous experience and knowledge of the world, responding thoughtfully to our feelings in the moment and communicating helpfully in supporting ourselves and others – these qualities can also be found in a truly 'integrated Adult' school.

Ultimately working towards autonomy in schools needs to be focused precisely on developing autonomous *schools*, not simply the promotion of autonomous relationships between a member of staff and their class or an individual pupil. Living autonomously is not just a good idea to use when thinking about pupil behaviour – it's a way of describing what is arguably the most effective position on which to build a whole-school ethos.

Finally, the purpose of moving towards autonomy – and indeed the basis of our writing this book – does not focus solely on helping schools become better places for children and adults to work together. It will be clear to readers that this book has not been written to simply help schools promote better behaviour in order to raise achievement. What we do as a society in bringing children and adults together in schools is give ourselves the opportunity to change the world for tomorrow. It is a massive investment of hope, one that we believe can sometimes be lost sight of in the busy life of the classroom or may be buried in internecine political struggles.

This book is not essentially about improving behaviour, raising grades, reconciling contrived political agendas or any other themes that can have a transient value. Our work is about what happens in classrooms and staffrooms, and how schools can provide hopeful opportunities for children and adults to work with one another. And in terms of developing an education system for this new millennium it is arguably the most important task tht goes on in our society:

> *Children are the living messages that we send to a future world that we will not see*
>
> (The Prophet, Kahil Gibran)

Developing a School Organisational Ego-gram

For each item, allocate a score to show how much each is true for the school. For each item where a score of 2 or 3 has been made, consider any evidence you have used in forming your decision:

Not true for the school	0	Moderately true for the school	2
Partly true for the school	1	Extremely true for the school	3

No.	Score	Statement
1		The school has an explicit code of conduct/discipline policy Evidence:
2		The school uses mediation systems for dealing with difficulties between pupils and/or staff Evidence:
3		The school complies with requirements and recommendations from external bodies e.g. LEA protocols, DfEE guidance etc. Evidence:
4		The school generally takes a sympathetic position to understanding pupils' problems Evidence:
5		The school enjoys contributing to a network of links with a wider professional and non-professional community, eg. local support agencies and community groups Evidence:
6		The school is explicit in demonstrating its sense of caring for pupils Evidence:
7		The school is effective in using systematic approaches to solving problems Evidence:
8		The school's expectations are clearly communicated to parents and pupils Evidence:

©Barrow et al. (2001)

No.	Score	Statement
9		Feelings are freely expressed by staff and pupils at the school Evidence:
10		The school provides a high level of courteousness/politeness in dealing with pupils and visitors Evidence:
11		The school takes contrary positions on issues relating to external requirements, for example OFSTED, LEA protocols Evidence:
12		The school is good at introducing/inducting new pupils and visitors Evidence:
13		The school is able to manage crisis calmly Evidence:
14		The school tends to seek information and support regarding new developments Evidence:
15		The school clearly enjoys its role and purpose as an organisation Evidence:
16		The school is regarded as a centre of good practice and other schools are encouraged to take note of its success Evidence:
17		The school is known for taking in pupils transferring/excluded from other schools Evidence:
18		The school responds best when visitors have regard for school protocol and etiquette Evidence:
19		The school maintains a problem solving approach, even under pressure Evidence:

©Barrow et al. (2001)

No.	Score	Statement
20		The school has a 'business-like' environment Evidence:
21		The school draws from previous experience when considering emerging difficulties Evidence:
22		The school is creative and inventive Evidence:
23		The school often intervenes in pupils' welfare arrangements Evidence:
24		The school can become over-involved pupil and staff personal situations Evidence:
25		The school expects the LEA/DfEE to set the school's terms of reference Evidence:
26		The school takes into account a range of perspectives when making decisions Evidence:
27		The school encourages both staff and pupils to test out their capabilities Evidence:
28		The school provides opportunities for staff and pupils to enjoy themselves Evidence:
29		The School expects clear direction from LEA, DfEE and OFSTED Evidence:
30		The school responds swiftly to requests and/or demands from external agencies, LEA/DfEE, parents Evidence:

©Barrow et al. (2001)

Step 1:   Transfer your scores to the summary below, against the question numbers and add up each column

Item	Score	Item	Score	Item	Score	Item	Score	Item	Score
1		4		2		3		5	
8		6		7		10		9	
16		12		13		11		14	
21		17		19		18		15	
23		24		20		25		22	
29		27		26		30		28	
Total		Total		Total		Total		Total	

Controlling Parent	Nurturing Parent	Adult	Adapted Child	Natural Child

Step 2:   Now draw a bar chart of the responses by marking horizontal lines at the score points

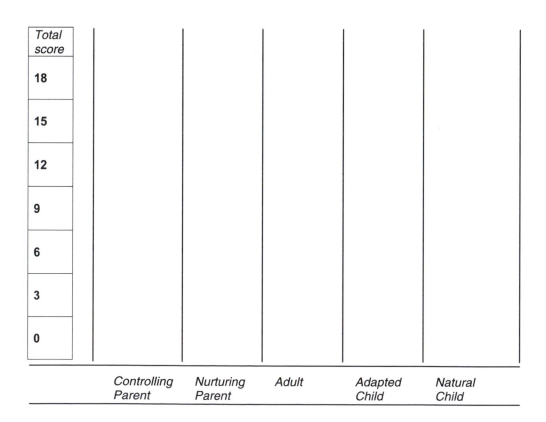

©*Barrow et al. (2001)*

Glossary of TA Terminology

accounting: a function of the Adult egostate, 'taking into account' all factors relevant to a situation, from both the external environment and internal Parent and Child input.

Adapted Child: one of the functional modes of interaction associated with the Child egostate. It can be positively cooperative or negatively complying or rebellious.

Adult: the Adult egostate which interacts with others from, and responds appropriately to, here-and-now reality.

affirmation: strokes which support people's need and ability to grow and develop; life-supporting messages linked to stages of development.

attribution: a defining message which tells someone they have a particular characteristic, e.g. stupid, clever etc., so that the person believes this of themselves.

autonomy: a state of being in the present characterised by awareness of self and others, and the ability to respond spontaneously with openness and authentic expression of feelings.

Child: the Child egostate, correctly a *set* of egostates which hold the behaviours, thinking and feeling experienced during the various stages of childhood.

complementary transaction: an interaction in which the egostate or mode addressed is the one which responds – hence on a transactional diagram the lines are parallel.

Compliant: one behavioural mode of Adapted Child, in which a person does what is asked or expected without regard to their own needs, wants or thinking.

contract: a bi- or multi-lateral negotiated agreement between parties to bring about a mutually determined outcome.

Controlling Parent: functional or behavioural mode of interacting with others which can be appropriately clear and limit-setting or inappropriately rigid and critical.

Cooperative: a positive behavioural mode, one aspect of Adapted Child, in which a person works well with others from autonomous choice.

Critical: a behavioural mode in which the person is domineering, authoritarian, rigid and/or critical.

crossed transaction: an interaction in which the response comes from an egostate or mode other than the one addressed; this may cause a break in communication which can be helpful if the interaction was previously 'stuck' or not beneficial.

cycles of development: a theory of human development and learning which includes recycling of developmental stages throughout life.

discounting: a process in which someone minimises, belittles or disregards some aspect of themselves, another person or the situation.

drama triangle: a way of describing and analysing psychological games; participants take on one or more of the three roles, Persecutor, Rescuer and Victim.

driver: an unhelpful and apparently compulsive way of behaving under stress. There are five: Be Perfect, Be Strong, Hurry Up, Please People and Try Hard. Also known as working styles when the positive aspects are emphasised, e.g. high standard of work (BP), calm in a crisis (BS) etc.

ego-gram: a histogram of egostate behaviours which shows the comparative time and energy spent on each.

egostate: a consistent pattern of feeling and experience and a corresponding consistent pattern of behaviour.

game (psychological game): a series of ulterior transactions which proceed to a predictable and familiar conclusion; usually results in bad feelings.

immature: negative behavioural mode of Natural Child in which a person exhibits egocentricity and disregard for others.

injunction: a self-limiting part of the script which causes us to believe we cannot do something, e.g. succeed, think, be important, be close to others; also known as *don'ts*.

life positions (windows on the world): four ways of seeing the world, related to perceptions of OK-ness in self and others. Also known as windows on the world as each offers a distinct perspective and excludes the others; also as *existential positions* because they are basic beliefs.

life-script (script): a set of beliefs and decisions made in childhood which continue to influence a person's life. Scripts include both self-limiting and self-protective beliefs and decisions; they can be updated as a person takes in new information, and they can be changed.

Marshmallow Parent: a behavioural mode in which someone is over-protective or 'smothering' towards another person.

mode: a behavioural aspect or manifestation of an egostate.

Natural Child: a functional or behavioural aspect of Child egostate which can be spontaneous and creative or selfish and immature.

nurture: a function of the Parent egostate.

Nurturing Parent: a functional aspect of Parent egostate and a behavioural mode in which interactions are caring and supportive.

OK-ness: the state of being in the I'm OK–You're OK life position.

Parent: an egostate which holds the thinking, feeling and ways of behaving derived from care-givers and other authority figures such as teachers.

permission: a message that something is OK, e.g. to think for oneself, to be close to others, to trust, to experience feelings.

Persecutor: a role on the drama triangle.

Rebellious: a behavioural mode, part of Adapted Child in which a person resists demands and refuses to cooperate.

recycling: the process of revisiting the stages of development experienced in childhood.

Rescuer: a role on the drama triangle.

script: see life-script.

Spontaneous: a behavioural mode, part of Natural Child, in which a person creatively expresses herself as she is.

stages of development: series of stages in which age-appropriate developmental tasks are achieved, or not; there are seven, including recycling in adulthood.

stroke: a unit of recognition, which may be positive or negative and for being (unconditional) or doing (conditional).

stroke economy: a set of social 'myths' or rules which limit the free and supportive giving and receiving of strokes.

structure: a function of the Parent.

Structuring Parent: a behavioural aspect of Controlling Parent in which someone interacts by providing direction, limit-setting and clarity of expectation.

three-cornered contract: a contract between any three parties in a situation; there may be other associated contracts.

transaction: an interaction consisting of a stimulus and a response.

Transactional Analysis: a system of theories, and their application, concerned with human development, personality, behaviour and communication, based on a philosophy of mutual and self-respect.

triangular contract: see three-cornered contract.

ulterior transaction: a transaction which takes place outside the participants' awareness and dictates the outcome of the interaction; the component of games.

Victim: a role on the drama triangle.

windows on the world: see life positions.

winners triangle: a positive way of behaving in interactions; developed from the 'well-intentioned' aspect of the drama triangle.

Further Reading

TA Today Ian Stewart and Vann Joines (Lifespace Publishing 1987)
The current classic reference book on TA, covering all the major concepts. Accessible and readable. Includes personal exercises to reinforce the theory.

Working it out at Work Julie Hay (Sherwood Publishing 1993)
Written for an organisational context, this book focuses on understanding relationships at work, but has much wider application. Easy to read and understand, it is an extremely clear explanation of TA theory as well as a means of learning about communication.

Esteem Builders Michelle Borba (Jalmar Press 1989)
An enormous resource book for teachers, containing hundreds of ideas and exercises for the classroom. Divided into sections covering five 'building blocks' of self-esteem; security, selfhood, affiliation, motivation and competence

Growing up Again Jean Illsley Clarke and Connie Dawson (Hazelden 1998)
A book on parenting, offering guidance on providing the structure and nurture children need for healthy development. Also very useful for teachers for understanding emotional development and self-esteem.

Tactics Rosemary Napper and Trudi Newton (TA Resources 2000)
Primarily intended as a resource and manual for adult educators based on TA. Teachers also find it useful and anyone involved in training or INSET will find many ideas for presenting material. Looks in detail at the process of learning.

TA for Kids Alvin Freed (Jalmar Press 1974)
Aimed at 10–13-year-olds, this is a good explanation of many TA ideas in a lively format. Just as useful for adults getting to know TA.

Born to Win Muriel James and Dorothy Jongeward (Addison Wesley 1971)
A TA classic with personal and group exercises, covering all the main ideas.

The Optimistic Child Martin Seligman (HarperCollins 1995)
Seligman is well known for the concept of 'learned helplessness'. This book presents the other side of the coin – optimism, too, can be learned through

authentic communication and problem solving. He believes effective learning leads to self-esteem, rather than the reverse.

The Scientist in the Crib Alison Gopnik *et al.* (Morrow 1999)
Recent, exciting publication on how babies and small children learn. Research based and very welcome to TA practitioners as there is much support for their observations and ideas.

TA in Education ed. George Adams (Ecrit 1990)
A collection of articles, from *Transactional Analysis Journal* and elsewhere, on using TA in teaching and learning.

Achieving Emotional Literacy Claude Steiner (Bloomsbury 1997)
By the originator of the concept of emotional literacy, discusses strokes and some other TA concepts in child rearing, relationships and work.

All these books are in print and can be obtained from good booksellers. In case of difficulty, or to obtain a full catalogue of TA books in print, and self-esteem materials, contact Kevin Smallwood, Charlton House, Dour Street, Dover CT16 1ED.

Information about training courses and conferences on TA can be obtained from the Institute of Transactional Analysis, by contacting: The Administrator, ITA, 6 Princes Street, Oxford OX4 1DD, admin@ita.org.uk.

Bibliography

Berne, E. (1961) *Transactional Analysis in Psychotherapy*. New York: Grove Press.

Berne, E. (1964) *Games People Play*. New York: Grove Press.

Borba, M. (1989) *Esteem Builders*. Torrance, Calif.: Jalmar Press.

Choy, A. (1990) 'The Winners Triangle', *Transactional Analysis Journal* **20**(1), 40–46.

Clarke, J. I. and Dawson, C. (1998) *Growing up Again*. Center City, Minn.: Hazelden.

Clarke, J. I. and Gesme, C. (1988) *Affirmation Ovals*. Minneapolis, Minn.: Daisy Press.

Crespelle, A. (1989) 'Le moi, le role et la personne: différences et interférences', *Actualités en Analyse Transactionnelle* **13**(52).

Department for Education and Employment (1999) *Social Inclusion: Pupil Support*. London: DfEE.

Department for Education and Employment (2000) *Draft Revised SEN Code of Practice*. London: DfEE.

Devlin, A. (1997) *Criminal Classes*. Winchester: Waterside.

Dieser, R. B. (1997) 'Empirical research on attribution theory', *Transactional Analysis Journal* **27**(3), 175–80.

English, F. (1975) 'The three-cornered contract', *Transactional Analysis Journal* **5**(4), 384–5.

Erikson, E. (1977) *Childhood and Society*. London: Paladin.

Galvin, P., Miller, A. and Nash, J. (1999) *Behaviour and Discipline in Schools: Devising and Revising a Whole-School Policy*. London: David Fulton Publishers.

Gesme, C. (1996) 'Helping children deal with feelings', *WE* **15**(2).

Goleman, D. (1996) *Emotional Intelligence*. London: Bloomsbury.

Gopnik, A., Meltzoff, A. N. and Kuhl, P. (1999) *The Scientist in the Crib*. New York: Morrow.

Hay, J. (1993) *Working it out at Work*. Watford: Sherwood Publishing.

Hay, J. (1995) *Donkey Bridges for Developmental TA*. Watford: Sherwood Publishing.

Hay, J. (1996) *Transactional Analysis for Trainers*. Watford: Sherwood Publishing.

Karpman, S. (1968) 'Fairy tales and script drama analysis', *Transactional Analysis Bulletin* 7(26), 39–43.

Lapworth, P., Sills, C. and Fish, S. (1995) *Transactional Analysis Counselling*. Bicester: Winslow Press.

Levin, P. (1982) 'The Cycle of Development', *Transactional Analysis Journal* 12(2), 129–39.

Montuschi, F. (1984) 'Teachers' scripts & in-service training programmes', *Transactional Analysis Journal* 14(1), 29–31.

Napper, R. and Newton, T. (2000) *Tactics*. Ipswich: TA Resources.

Piaget, J. (1973) *The Child's Conception of the World*. London: Paladin.

Qualifications and Curriculum Authority/Department for Education and Employment (2000) *Supporting School Improvement: emotional and behavioural development*. London: QCA/DfEE.

Rogers, C. (1978) *On Personal Power*. London: Constable.

Steiner, C. (1971) 'The stroke economy', *Transactional Analysis Journal* 1(3), 9–15.

Steiner, C. (1974) *Scripts People Live*. New York: Grove Press.

Steiner, C. (1977) *A Fuzzy Tale*. Torrance, Calif.: Jalmar Press.

Steiner, C. (1997) *Achieving Emotional Literacy*. London: Bloomsbury.

Steiner, C. (2001) Personal communication.

Stern, D. (1998) *Diary of a Baby*. New York: Basic Books.

Stewart, I. and Joines, V. (1987) *TA Today*. Nottingham: Lifespace Publishing.

Teacher Training Agency (1999) *National SEN Specialist Standards*. London: TTA.

Temple, S. (1999a) 'Functional fluency for educational transactional analysts', *Transactional Analysis Journal* 29(3), 164–74.

Temple, S. (1999b) 'Teaching with TA', *Institute of Transactional Analysis* 54(2), 24–5.

Temple, S. (2000) 'The stroke management map', *Institute of Transactional Analysis* 56(1), 24–5.

University of Birmingham (1998) *Emotional and Behavioural Difficulties in Mainstream Schools*. London: DfEE.

Watkins, C. and Wagner, P. (2000) *Improving School Behaviour*. London: Paul Chapman.

Index